The Soviet Administration in Northern Transylvania

(November 1944 – March 1945)

THE SOVIET ADMINISTRATION IN NORTHERN TRANSYLVANIA

(November 1944 – March 1945)

By

MARCELA SĂLĂGEAN

English Translation by
ROBERT MIHAI ROSCA

EAST EUROPEAN MONOGRAPHS, BOULDER
DISTRIBUTED BY COLUMBIA UNIVERSITY PRESS, NEW YORK

2002

EAST EUROPEAN MONOGRAPHS, NO. DXCVIII

ISBN 0-88033-496-7
Library of Congress Control Number 2002108608

Printed in the United States of America

CONTENTS

Chapter ... Page

Introduction ... 7

Chapter 1
THE ARMISTICE ... 11

Chapter 2
PROJECTS OF THE GREAT POWERS REGARDING THE FUTURE OF TRANSYLVANIA ... 27

Chapter 3
NORTHERN TRANSYLVANIA UNDER ROMANIAN ADMINISTRATION (SEPTEMBER – NOVEMBER 1944) ... 39

Chapter 4
THE SOVIET ADMINISTRATION IN NORTHERN TRANSYLVANIA (NOVEMBER 1944 – MARCH 1945) ... 65

- The Gendarmerie ... 77
- The statute of the ethnic minorities ... 81
- The presence of the Soviet forces in northern Transylvania ... 95
- The Law ... 105
- The condition of the Economy ... 107
- The medical service condition ... 112
- The education ... 114
- The political situation ... 119
- Maramureş ... 125

Chapter 5
THE REESTABLISHMENT OF THE ROMANIAN ADMINISTRATION IN NORTHERN TRANSYLVANIA ... 141

Conclusion ... 151

Bibliography ... 153

Appendices ... 165

INTRODUCTION

By the end of the summer of 1940, upon decision of the second arbitration from Vienna, Transylvania has been divided between Hungary and Romania by tracing an artificial frontier which practically rendered void both the historical identity and the authentic and long strengthened historical tradition of this province. Through adopting this unviable solution, the nazi Germany and the fascist Italy were deliberately transforming the Transylvanian problem into a hotbed of local instability and an object of competition between Romania and Hungary; problem that leaded to increase the subordination of these two countries to the policy of the Third Reich. A few years later, the Soviet dictator Iosif Vissarionovici Stalin took advantage, in his turn, of the existence of this source of instability in order to enforce control over the two countries, by means of a series of actions in which Transylvania has often been used as a swap coin and a means to blackmail.

During the years that followed the World War II, the policy of the Great Powers regarding the problem of Transylvania has often become object of interest for the historiography, which analysed, in various degrees of objectivity, the ways in which the Allies have tried to neutralize this source of tensions in Central Europe.

Before proceeding to treat of the proposed subject, we consider that a few historiographical details might be helpful.

There is a pretty small number of studies in the Romanian historiography dedicated to the subject that we shall try to analyse in the present study. Prior to 1989, the problem of the northern Transylvania's statute between September 1944 and March 1945 has been treated dogmatically and tangentially, and the historians interested in it were short of real possibilities of documentation and were conditioned, at the same time, by a very narrow ideology. The main part of the historiographical studies were treating on the moment of the Vienna resolution (dated August the 30th 1940) and on the development of the military operations during the World War II, with regard to some elements standing for preamble and consequences.

Since 1990, however, as the access to the documentary sources has been opened, the number of studies concerning this subject has grown significantly, even though a certain attitude of reserve when considering the northern Transylvania's specific problems may be detected. It was of a particular use for me to consult some studies that analyse the attitude of the Great Powers towards Transylvania during the final period of the Second World War and the period of preparation for the Peace Conference or some particular details in connection with the presence of the Red Army in Romania. A large series of other studies concerning that period are either synthesis studies or collection of documents, the authors of which, even if referring to Romania as a whole, were still able to offer us information or interpretations worthy to be taken into consideration. All these studies are gathered in a general bibliography in the final part of this work.

The lack of extensive studies focused on the complex and specific problems of northern Transylvania is compensated, in a way, by the large number of articles published both in magazines dedicated to the public and in specialized periodical publications. These sources of documentation have the merit of bringing valuable information of a great diversity in the scientific circulation, coming from archives or from the memoirs of the personalities contemporary with those events.

As a consequence, the main part of the information that lies at the basis of this study has been obtained by consulting the archive funds from The National Archive, the archives of the Ministry of Foreign Affairs and of the Ministry of Interior, The Archive of The Chairmanship of the Council of Ministers and especially from the districts archive – all of these providing us valuable documents. In addition to the unpublished information obtained by consulting the documents, we have used notes from the press of that time, known as it is that journalism can be the show of the spirit tendencies of a community in a particular age.

One of the reasons that made us dedicate our efforts to this subject was the absence of a study that would analyse the complex problem of northern Transylvania as a whole in the lapse of time starting from the liberation of this territory to its administratively restitution to Romania – as a result of the installation of the government of Dr. Petru Groza, in Bucharest.

Relying on the documentary sources mentioned above, we considered that it would be right to structure the present study into five chapters that would analyse, altogether with the presentation of the historical context of the developments, the political and administrative situation established in northern Transylvania in November 1944.

This approach, though quite difficult due to the lack of a theoretical and practical pattern of broaching such a research, has benefited from the priceless help generously offered by the professors from The Modern History and The Contemporary History Departaments of the University «Babeş – Bolyai» from Cluj-Napoca and by the specialists from the Archives of Cluj-Napoca, Bistriţa, Târgu-Mureş, Baia Mare and from The Ministry of Foreign Affairs. Also, I would like to thank the Centre for Transylvanian Studies from Cluj-Napoca, respectable institution that gave me, along all these years, the support that I needed to accomplish this research project. My thanks head also to «The Foundation for an Open Society» which offered me the oportunity to benefit by a generous young scholars support programme.

I would also like to thank to the one person who made possible the publishing of this study in English, Professor Stephen Fischer-Galaţi. My humble thoughts of gratitude are insufficient to express my feelings in their plenitude.

And, last but not least, I thank my husband for his support, encouraging and understanding.

Realizing that we have exhausted a few general problems through this approach, we still leave room, at the same time, for new researchs that would study thoroughly the diversity of the subjects that we have brouched here. However, we hope that our writing will offer to anyone interested in it a view over a less studied subject in the Romanian historiography

CHAPTER ONE

THE ARMISTICES

The evening of the 23rd of August 1944, The Proclamation of King Mihai I announced the overthrow of the regime of Antonescu, the withdrawal of Romania out of the alliance with the powers of the Axis and the ceasing of warfare against the antifascist coalition. At the same time, the Romanian Army got the order to cease all military operations against the Soviet forces and to retreat south of the strategic line Focşani – Nămoloasa – Galaţi, allowing thus the Red Army to make a giant leap towards West. Despite the reestablishement of the constitutional regime, of the political pluralism and the democratical liberties, there were not few those who regarded with anxiety the Soviet display of forces on Romanian territory. Anyway, few people have guessed the real size of the disaster to come. For Romania, hard times were about to follow, incomparably worse times than those of the previous six years of consecutive dictatorships, the first sign being represented by the fast and brutal ascent of one party – the communist party – that was, in fact, a fifth column in the service of the power that was to be recognized as an absolute ruler of Central and Eastern Europe by the percentages from Moscow.

Short after the 23rd of August 1944, the new government, lead by General Constantin Sănătescu, has received the confirmation of the terms of armistice from Novikov, the Soviet ambassador in Cairo, terms offered to Romania, as far back as April 1944, with the supplements agreed at Stockholm, which included the provision of the establishment of a free zone reserved to the functioning of the Romanian government, in order to ensure the existence of the Romanian state as an independent political entity. This accepting had been, however, a matter of pure conjuncture, and the international situation of Romania changed radically when Great Britain and the United States, listening to the insistences of the Soviet Union, have agreed on the signing of the Moscow Armistice only by Romania and the Soviet Union, the latter as sole representative of the allied powers. The Soviet Union is not the only one to be taken into consideration for the delay of the signing of the armistice, as it has been usually asserted until now. Great Britain has had a major contribution to this, by invoking the necessity of obtaining the agreement of the dominions on the modifications added to the text of the armistice, on London initiative. However, the Soviet government and the Red Army have exploited at its utmost this confused «neither peace, nor war» situation[1], in a manner too well-known to need any further commentss. The Armistice Convention, signed only on the 12th of September 1944, when the Red Army ,from a military point of view ,already controlled the situation in Romania, did no longer include any provision on the existence of a Soviet free zone. In addition, in its text, the references to the Allied High Command were followed, between parentheses, by the specification ***Soviet***, a detail which indicated in a very transparent manner who has the power and the authority to decide in the Romanian matters[2].

The firm belief that Germany is going to lose the war and that Romania will have to detach from it has been felt as far back as the end of 1942, but especially beginning with 1943, at the same time as the Germans have lost the strategic initiative on the Soviet battle-front. Still, the rulers of the country in that period have kept on delaying the breaking off the alliance with Berlin, hoping to conclude a favourable armistice with the Allies. The following developments and the situation on the battle-front in the early summer of 1944 have required the political elements in Bucharest the adoption of some fast solutions to prevent the transformation of the Romanian territory in a battleground. In such conditions, the forming of a coalition against Germany and, implicitly, against the military regime of Marshal Ion Antonescu has imposed itself immediately ,but been acomplished with quite some difficulty because of the justified attitude of reserve of the traditional parties regarding the collaboration with the communist party.

Among the most important goals of the government of General Constantin Sănătescu, figured the regulation of the international juridical statute of Romania in the recent situation and the liberation of the territory occupied by Hungary as a result of the Vienna Award from the 30th of August 1940. In the lapse of time before the signing of the Armistice Convention and in the following period, the government has carried on an intense diplomatic activity with these ends in view. In fact, the most ardent concern of the Romanian government has been that of signing as quickly as possible the armistice with the Allies, as to confer legality to the recent international statute of the country, the statute of an ally in the war against Germany. On the 25th of August 1944, the Moscow radio station had broadcasted the declaration of the Foreign Affairs Soviet Commissary regarding Romania. On this occasion, the U.S.S.R. renewed the promise that they «do not intend to acquire any part of the Romanian territory or to change the existing social order of Romania»[3]. In order to sign the armistice, it has been constituted a delegation, in which there were taking part, among others, Lucreţiu Pătrăşcanu, Gheorghe Pop, Dumitru Dămăceanu, Prince Ştirbei etc., delegation that has arrived in Moscow on the 30th of August 1944[4]. At the head of the delegation has been appointed Lucreţiu Pătrăşcanu, in hope of obtaining more reasonable conditions. It was the same conviction, proven to be false, as in the First World War, when it was thought that the presence of a Germanophile conservative, Alexandru Marghiloman, at the head of the government would diminish the rigours of the peace treaty stipulations. Then, in 1944, again, it was considered that by entrusting to a communist the leadership of the delegation, Moscow would be more benevolent. Sir Archibald Clark Kerr, the British Ambassador in Moscow, has understood the drama of Lucreţiu Pătrăşcanu when he realized how illusory the plans made by Bucharest were: «He had come here convinced of the fact that, as a communist, he would find immediately the key to the Russians' hearts and would unlock the door to a more clement armistice... This is a mistake in which many people are falling and Pătrăşcanu was not to be blamed, because there was nobody in Romania who could say to him that his hopes were vain»[5]. After many long days of awaiting, the Romanian delegation has been met by Molotov on September the 10th and has been confronted with an already drawn up text of the Armistice Convention[6]. After receiving the document, the Romanian delegation has asked for a one day delay, in order to examine the twenty points of the convention, so that the negotiations began on September the 11th 1944. Clark Kerr, the Ambassador of Great Britain and Averell

Harriman[7], the U.S. Ambassador have participated to these discussions, but they have had a neutral attitude.

The deliberate delay of the signing of the amistice has had as a consequence the occupation of a large part of the Romanian territory by the Red Army, which allowed Stalin and Molotov to dictate conditions to Romania. In a telegram dated August the 31st 1944, Grigore Niculescu Buzeşti expressed his concern on the delay of the signing of the armistice by the Soviets: «The Soviet Army in Romania proceeds on its advance, probably with the purpose of occupying as much as possible, if not all our territory, on pretext that the armistice hasn't been signed yet, even though the advance of the Soviet forces in Romania is in no respect justified, considering the fact that the Romanian government has wiped out by now all the German centers of resistance, entirely by his own forces. The public opinion is very seriously concerned about this situation and there are rumours that the signing of the armistice is being delayed precisely for the Soviet forces to get into Romanian territory»[8].

The delegation sent to Moscow for the conclusion of the armistice has received on September the 4th a report on the abuses of the Soviet Army, which acted as if in an occupancy regime. The second point of the report specified that: «...the Soviet forces act, in many cases, as if in an occupancy regime... The ammunition and military equipment stores of the Romanian Army have been taken over...Also, the Romanian Army and authorities are required for important conscriptions of equipment... Direct and substantial requisitions of vehicles, horses, waggons, cattle and food have been performed, fact that paralyses the activity of our Army, the functioning of the state administration and the economic life»[9]. Under such conditions, the very zone which was supposed to be left unoccupied according to the previous agreements, passed unperceived. Consecuently, insistent claims that the Soviet forces would stop at least by the river Olt appeared, as the signing of the armistice became then a pressing matter, the delay of which would have prejudiced the prestige of the country[10]. The sovereignty of the state has been violated up to the point that the German prisoners or the political ones have been taken by force by the Russian officers from the custody of the Romanian authorities.

This was the frame of the circumstances by the time of the signing of the Armistice Convention. Soviet forces had already occupied much of Romania, acting as if in a hostile territory, fact that created an unfavourable impression among the population.

The armistice has been signed in Moscow on the 12th of September 1944. Molotov was presiding. Harriman, the U.S.A.'s ambassador and Clark Kerr, the British ambassador were also present. In the telegram sent to Washington, Harriman described the manner in which these discussions were taking place: Molotov read each stipulation, then allowed the Romanian delegation to say what they have to say, ignoring what they have just said and passing on to the next stipulation. At the same time, he noticed that the Romanians seemed less anxious about the stipulations themselves than about the way in which they could be interpreted[11]. The Armistice Convention, meant to regulate the international situation of Romania, established, in fact a regime of Soviet occupation (general's Cortlandt Van Rensselaer Schuyler words). The American representative in the Allied Control Commission in Romania were persuaded that the majority of the Convention's articles had a distinct Soviet perfume, but all provisions were to be put into practice by the Romanian government under the attentive supervision of the Allied Control Commission. In this regard, the eighteenth article of the Armistice Convention stipulated: «An Allied Control Commission will be created and will take over the regulation and the control of the execution of the present conditions, until the end of the war, under the general command and the orders of the Allied High Command (Soviet), that acts on behalf of the Allied Powers»[12].

The Armistice Convention, with its 20 points, settled the obligation that Romania had to the Allies, especially to the Soviet Union, obligation reflected in the political and the economic life and in administration. For this reason, the Convention represented for a while the fundamental document upon which the relations between Romania and the Soviet state were based. In this respect, we find necessary to enumerate its most important stipulations: the carrying on of the warfare alongside the Allies, with 12 divisions; the confinement of the Germans and Hungarian citizens existent in the country; ensuring the movement of the troops in the territory; the liberation of the prisoners and the abrogation of the nazi laws; the dissolution of the pro-Hitlerite organizations; the cooperation with the Soviet High Command for the arresting and condemnation of the war criminals; Soviet censorship of the publications, movies, entertainment and communications; the reestablishment of the Romanian administration behind the battlefield at a distance of at least 50 – 100 km; the decision of the Vienna Award was declared null and void, the governments of the Allies stating their approval for the return of Transylvania (or of most of it) to Romania, return that was about to become final with the confirmation of the Peace Conference; an Allied Control Commission, which was supposed to monitor the carrying out of the conditions, had been created. For all that, Romania's statute of co-belligerent nation had not recognized [13].

Right after the resuming of the relations with the Soviet Union, it can be asserted that Romania was put in a position of inferiority. As a result of the well-known percentage agreement, that took place between Stalin and Churchill, Romania was placed in the Soviet sphere of influence. Harriman foresaw, right after the signing of the armistice, that the agreement would offer the Russians «unlimited control over the economic life of Romania and, at the same time, a police power during the period of the armistice»[14]. The disappointement that followed the signing of such a document was expressed clearly by the large majority of the Romanian politicians. For exemple, Iuliu Maniu was declaring: «Is this an armistice? It would have been better if we did not signed it. It is a military occupation and by no means an armistice»[15].

Even in that form full of disadvantages for the Romanian side, the text of the Convention has been violated countless times. The country was practically under the domination of the Allied Control Commission, where the Soviets were so powerful that they could decide all by themselves in any situation. The 18th article, for example, stipulated the forming of the Allied Control Commission with the representatives of the three Powers, but the actual decision was taken by the Soviet High Command, that acted in the name of the Allied Powers. That meant that the entire control of its application was entrusted to a Soviet commission, where the British and the American representatives were at the Soviets discretion. For instance, the British and the American citizens were not allowed to travel in Romania without a leave from the Soviet. The 19th article, as it had been formulated, created the possibility of a blackmail in the problem of Transylvania, allowing thus Moscow to interfere in Romania's internal politics.

The signing of the armistice did not solved the ambiguity created by the military occupation of the country, whose real nature Moscow has avoided for a long time to recognize, by duplicity and lack of information and with the help of the communist press and propaganda. The Western governments have been informed about this situation by a telegraphic report send on the 27th of September 1944 from Bucharest to London, by the British expert in Romania of the Allied Control Commission, Melville. That telegram informed that the signing of the armistice has not brought what the population and the politicians have expected and that the public opinion was expecting the Americans and the British to get more involved in Romania. In fact, the things did not turn out the way expected the majority of the elements of Romanian society expected [16]. A huge discrepancy has been created between the international political and juridical statute ***de jure*** and ***de facto*** of Romania, in the way that, according to the armistice, Romania was considered to be an independent state, with a number of limitations and restrictions stipulated in the 3rd, the 14th, the 16th, the 17th and the 18th articles. In reality, Romania had a statute of an occupied country, with the main attributes of sovereignty and independence usurped by the Soviet occupation authorities[17].

The presence of the Soviet soldiers in Romania until 1958 can be divided into three separate periods of time, each with its own characteristics and ends[18]. The first period is the one between April and May 1944 (when the German – Romanian forces have lost their defensive positions on the river Dniester) and the signing of the armistice[19]. During all this period of time, almost all the territory of Moldavia was under the control of the Soviet forces. A Soviet military administration has been established in northern Moldavia, southern Bukovina and Bessarabia, while for the rest of the country, the Romanian military and civil administration was controlled by the Soviets. The Soviet presence in Romania was marked by a regime of terror, violence, robbery without discrimination since the beginning, but became systematic afterwards. The food reserve, the means of traction, the tools and the equipment has been put in hand to the occupation forces, which were sending them over the border[20]. The British military and political authorities have received information on these events by the middle of September 1944, from various sources. The Western governments prefered, though, to consider these reports as being influenced by the German disinformation service or by the ironguardists infiltrated in Romania in order to provoke confusion and instigate conflicts between Romanians and the Soviets[21] . Reffering to this situation, Constantin Titel Petrescu stated, during the meeting of the Council of Ministers on the 25th of September 1944, that: «I got a report about the missing of the Romanian authorities in those territories. It seems that even Dobrudja is no longer part of the country. Our authorities have left»[22] . General Dumitru Dămăceanu reached to the same conclusion, after an inspection in the territory, ordered by the chairman of the Council of Ministers. During the meeting of the cabinet, on the 26th of September 1944, he concluded: «Today, I can say that Moldavia has been separated from the rest of the country, for certain reasons. The Soviets have cut off the phone and telegraph lines and have confiscated the radios in these territories. They have changed, too, the rail gauge from Ungheni to Iaşi, Paşcani and Ploieşti, and from Cernăuţi to Focşani, so that the Romanian rail freightage is completely paralysed between the rivers Siret and Prut»[23] .

The second period of the Soviet occupation is the one between the signing of the armistice and the conclusion of the Peace Treaty. Until the complete liberation of the Romanian territory from the German – Hungarian forces, on October the 25th 1944, the Soviets have justified the presence of their forces in Romania by pure military reasons. When the Soviet and the Romanian forces have crossed the border, the Soviets have alleged that their military presence would not last much longer. The Romanian authorities have consistently required the Allied Control Commission additional explanations on the presence in the country of such a great number of Soviet soldiers. The responses were evasive and they were followed by no precise action leading to the settlement of this problem[24] .

The situation has become more alarming when Soviet divisions have been stationed in the strategic areas of the country and the Romanian government has been given the order to reduce significantly its military effectives in the country. On the 30th of November 1944, Constantin Sănătescu required explanations to the Allied Control Commission and especially to General Vladislav Vinogradov about the violation of the Armistice Convention with respect to the transportation and the stationing of the Soviet forces in Romania. Receiving no satisfactory response, later on, General Nicolae Rădescu, the Prime

Minister of the time, addressed to the Allied Control Commission on the 9th of December 1944, requiring the removal of the Soviet forces from the Romanian territories, due to the fact that their presence was illegal and violated the stipulations of the armistice. Using an aggressive tone, Vladislav Vinogradov responded, on the 12th of December 1944, to the Romanian government that the stationing of the Soviet forces tallies with the 3rd article of the armistice; the Romanian government and Headquarters will provide favourable conditions to the Soviet and Allied forces for their free circulation within Romanian territory, in any direction, if requested by the military situation. Also, the Romanian government and Headquarters had to ensure, at their own expense, the shifting of the Soviet Army, by land, by sea or by air[25].

An important goal of the Soviets in Romania was that of imposing direct or indirect control over the institutions of the state, especially those authorized by the Constitution to defend the independence, the sovereignty and the social order: the army, the police, the gendarmerie, and the Law. The annihilation of the Army has begun as early as the first days after the 23rd of August 1944, when thousands of experienced officers and soldiers were taken prisoners, the effectives of the Romanian Army being thus drastically diminished. This action of the Soviet has had the support of the communist press, which was leading a vehement campaign of discrediting the Romanian Army. The result was that of lowering even more the soldiers spirits[26].

In a letter addressed to Vishinsky on the 15th of November 1944, referring to the impact produced on the Romanian public opinion by the demobilization of numerous divisions, the president of the National Peasant Party indicated that: «These measures, which are not in accordance with the stipulations of the armistice, have been accepted by the Romanian government only under the threat of disarming the Romanian troops by the Soviet forces, even if, unlike Finland, the armistice with Romania did not include such a stipulation»[27].

After adopting measures according to which the Romanian Army would become a symbolical presence inside Romania, the Allied Control Commission has passed on to reduce and modify the structure of the police, of the gendarmerie and of the firefighters brigades. By the order V-243 of November the 25th 1944, addressed to the Council of Ministers, Marshal R.I. Malinovsky requested the reduction of the gendarmerie units' effectives. Also, on the 1st of December 1944, the

Allied Control Commission has sent to Bucharest a project for the territorial reorganization of the local Commands of the gendarmerie units in the country[28]. The police and the gendarmerie forces in the great cities have been reduced, the remaining ones being insufficient to maintain the public safety and order. The Romanian authorities have objected to these abuses, claiming that these measures are contravening to the 1st and the 17th articles of the Armistice Convention, but, obviously, the objections were without result.

The Romanian government has created the institutions and the structures needed, at the center or locally, to render possible the application of the stipulations of the Armistice Convention. The Allied Control Commission already existed, as a structure holding discretionary powers, strictly supervised by the Soviet. The 18th article of the Convention specified that it will be established an Allied Control Commission, which will assume the regulation and the control of the execution of the present stipulations, under the general command and the orders of the Allied High Command, on behalf of the Allied Powers[29]. In the appendix of this article were added the following specifications: «The Romanian government and its authorities will fulfil all the orders of the Allied Control Commission that result from the Armistice Convention. The Allied Control Commission will establish structures or departments, authorizing them to execut various functions. In addition to that, the Allied Control Commission will be allowed to have officials in different parts of Romania»[30].

For the fulfilment of these obligations it was created an appropriate commission, The Romanian Commission for the Application of the Armistice. Thus, on the 24th of October 1944, it has been signed the decree concerning «the establishment, the organization and the functioning of the Commission for the Application of the Armistice between Romania and the United Nations»[31]. The purpose of the new established institution (formed of five members and a chairman, appointed through royal decree, at the proposal of the Foreign Affairs Minister) was that of ensuring a permanent contact with the Allied Control Commission. The decisions of the Romanian Commission for the Application of the Armistice were transmitted for execution to the Romanian public authorities and institutions, any other authority of the state being obliged to require notification from this commission. The importance given to the Romanian Commission for the Application of the Armistice results from the provisions of the sixth article, which established that all demands to be forwarded will be given priority at the government.

To the decree-law reffering to the purpose and the functioning of the Romanian Commission for the Application of the Armistice have been adjoined, by the Sănătescu and Rădescu governments, a series of addings. As a result of the approach made by general Aurel Aldea, the Minister of the Internal Affairs, on the 27th of October 1944, a decision[32] has been adopted, regarding the establishment and the competence of the Service for the Application of the Convention of Armistice, its most important prerogative being that of studying the provisions of the Armistice Convention, «the execution of which is devolved upon the Ministry of the Internal Affairs»[33] . For the purpose of stimulating the activity of the Service for the Application of the Armistice Convention, the administrative chief inspector Corneliu Popescu has been named its «guide» and, at the same time, mandatory of the Ministry of the Internal Affairs[34] to the Romanian Commission for the Application of the Armistice. On the same occasion, general Marcel Moşoiu has been commissioned with the leadership of the new created service[35] .

On the 22nd of December 1944, responding to an initiative of Constantin Vişoianu, the Minister of the Foreign Affairs, the King has signed the Law no.654, according to which the prerogatives of the Romanian Commission for the Application of the Armistice and those of its chairman were more clearly defined. New institutions subordinated to the commission have appeared. The transformation was obvious from the very first article, which comprised points that specified the competence of the commission. These prerogatives were: a) to offer the interpretation of the Armistice Convention, according to the main standards determined by the Council of Ministers; b) to provide guidance, norms and instructions for the execution of the Armistice Convention; c) to supervise the execution of the stipulations of the Armistice Convention[36] . The second article, too, brought a modification, by the fact that the number of the members of the Romanian Commission for the Application of the Armistice increasead from 5 to 6. The content of the next article was also interesting, allowing to be created and to function, in addition to this commission, advisory commissions or permanent commissions, in conformity with the chairman's decision, commissions that would have special competence and external services, also[37]. Taking into account the fact that the chairman of the Romanian Commission for the Application of the Armistice had to resolve an excessive number of problems, he was offered the possibility to bestow on one or more members of the commission or on general secretaries the prerogative of resolving parts of the current working[38]. It is worth mentioning the fact that the Romanian Commission for the Application of the Armistice alone could receive the requests of the Allied High Command and those of the Allied Control Commission, and had the obligation to resolve these requests, in close co-operation with the authorities and the institutions of the Romanian state. Another decree-law for the reorganization of the Romanian Commission for the Application of the Armistice has been signed by King Mihai I on the 17th of April 1945 and the Prime Minister Petru Groza has justified this new decree-law by the necessity of creating new structures which would assume the task of a better supervision of the execution of the Armistice Convention[39]. It was thought that, by constituting a delegation of the commission's general secretaries, it would be realized a more close and permanent relation with the Romanian Commission for the Application of the Armistice, and the measures taken for the execution of the armistice stipulations would be carried out under direct supervision[40]. The concern for a functioning as rigorous as possible of the Romanian Commission for the Application of the Armistice is obvious, from which it was expected, especially during the first months after the signing of the armistice, to limit the Soviet insistences concerning the carrying out of the stipulations, permitting a better functioning of the economic and administrative structures of the state. Also, for the execution of the Armistice Convention, an economic department was established , having «the prerogative to prepare the statistic data and information required for the economic documentation»[41].

Violating the Armistice Convention's stipulations that insured the independence and the sovereignty of Romania (art.1) and the reestablishment of the civil administration in the entire Romanian territory (art.17), the abusive conduct of the Soviet military authorities has obstructed by force the Romanian government to extend its administration over the entire country[42]. Two months after the signing of the armistice and after the ceasing of the military operation in Romania, the government has been obstructed to exert its administrative prerogatives, not only in northern Transylvania, but also in southern Bukovina, northern Moldavia and Dobrudja. These territories were controlled and administrated abusively by the Soviet High Command. The improvised administration has passed on to carry out social and economic reforms in these regions.

As a result of the discussions with Marshal Malinovsky, I. Christu, the chairman of the Romanian Commission for the Application of the Armistice has got on the 25th of September 1944 the leave to install Romanian administrators in Moldavia, southern Bukovina and Dobrudja. According to this agreement, the Romanian government has sent on the 24th of October 1944 a train with soldiers and civilians in northern Moldavia and southern Bukovina, ready to take over its duties; this train, however, has been kept for a few weeks, by the Russians, in the railway station of Adjud. For exemple, in Huşi, by the end of November 1944, the administration was still under the direct control of the local Soviet Command[43].

An entire legislation would rise from the necessity to accomplish the stipulations of the Armistice Convention and a bureacratical network belonging to the Allied Control Commission will cover the Romanian territory, annuling or altering the prerogatives and the decisions of the legitimate national institutions and structures. The Allied (Soviet) High Command and the Allied Control Commission have become two efficient official instruments within the Romanian territory and the introduction of the term ***Soviet*** in the denominations of the two institutions implies, certainly, the political-ideological meaning and content of the term's utilization and of the regime appealed to apply this convention[44]. The Allied Control Commission will become, in time, a structure that parasitized the functioning of the state apparatus, the Romanian officials shaping their decisions and their actions according to the demands of the commission's representatives[45].

NOTES:

[1] Florin Constantiniu, «*O istorie sinceră a poporului român*», Ed. Univers Enciclopedic, Bucharest, 1997, pp 444

[2] Nicole Ciachir, « *Marile puteri şi România, (1856 – 1947)*», Ed. Albatros, Bucharest, 1996, pp 326

[3] « *România – marele sacrificat al celui de-al doilea război mondial. Documente*», vol.I, editor Marin Radu Mocanu, Bucharest, 1994, pp 261

[4] Nicolae Baciu, «*Agonia României, 1944 – 1948. Dosarele secrete acuză*», ed.Dacia, Cluj-Napoca, 1990; Gheorghe Buzatu, «*România cu şi fără Antonescu. Documente, studii, relatări si comentarii*», ed. Moldova, Iaşi, 1991, pp 283

[5] Florin Constantiniu, *op. cit.*, pp 444

[6] Vlad Georgescu, «*Istoria românilor de la origini până în zilele noastre* », the third edition, ed. Humanitas, Bucharest, 1992, pp 251

[7] Gheorghe Buzatu, *op. cit.*, pp 251-252

[8] *Romania, marele sacrificat...*, pp 275

[9] *Ibidem*, pp 283

[10] *Ibidem*, pp 284

[11] Ivor Porter, «*Operaţiunea <<Autonomus>> în România în vreme de război*», ed. Humanitas, Bucharest, 1991, pp 294

[12] Maria Ignat, «*Implicaţiile Convenţiei de Armistiţiu asupra evoluţiei vieţii politice româneşti*», in «*6 martie 1945. Începuturile comunizării României*», ed. Enciclopedică, Bucharest, 1995

[13] «*Convenţia de armistiţiu*» in « *România, marele sacrificat...*»

[14] Vlad Georgescu, *op. cit.*, pp 242

[15] Nicolae Baciu, *op. cit.*, pp 273

[16] Constantin Hlihor, Ioan Scurtu, «*The Red Army in Romania*», The Center for Romanian Studies, Iasi, Oxford, Portland, 2000, pp 34

[17] *Ibidem.*

[18] *Ibidem*, pp 35

[19] *Ibidem.*

[20] *Ibidem.*

[21] *Ibidem.*

[22] *Ibidem.*

[23] *Ibidem*; see also Gheorghe Onişoru, «*România în anii 1944 – 1948. Transformări economice şi realităţi sociale*», Fundaţia Academia Civică, 1998

[24] *Ibidem*, pp 36

[25] *Ibidem*, pp 38

[26] *Ibidem*, pp 48

[27] *Ibidem*, pp 50

[28] *Ibidem*, pp 51

[29] «*Monitorul Oficial*», 1944, nr.219, pp 6374

[30] *Ibidem.*

[31] *Ibidem.*

[32]*Ibidem*, no. 256, pp 7152 – 7153

[33] *Ibidem.*

[34] *Ibidem.*

[35] *Ibidem.*

[36] *Ibidem*, no.298, pp 8372

[37] *Ibidem.*

[38] *Ibidem.*

[39] *Ibidem*, 1945, no.90, pp 3212

[40] *Ibidem*, pp 3210 – 3212

[41] *Ibidem.*

[42] Constantin Hlihor, Ioan Scurtu, *op. cit.*, pp 51

[43] *Ibidem*, pp 52

[44] Flori Stănescu, Dragoş Zamfirescu, «*Ocupaţia sovietică în România. Documente 1944 – 1946*», ed. Vremea, Bucharest, 1998, pp 9

[45] *Ibidem.*

CHAPTER TWO

PROJECTS OF THE GREAT POWERS CONCERNING THE FUTURE OF TRANSYLVANIA

The problem of the future statute of Transylvania had been a concern for the diplomacy of the allies as early as in 1942 – 1943, when the certainty of the victory over the Powers of the Axis began to shape. Of course, the decisions of the Second Dictate from Vienna, considered to be an expression of the German domination programme over Central Europe, had not been recognized, at the time, by any of the Western governments. Nonetheless, released from any obligation to Romania as a result of the fact that it joined the war and confronted, also, with the evidence that there really was a Transylvanian problem, Great Britain and the U.S.A. did their best to identify the most judicious solutions needed for its solving. In this way, it have been taken into account, practically, all the possible alternatives: the division of this province, its complete restoration to one of the states that claimed it, its autonomy or its independence as part of a larger confederation. Thus, it is not surprising the fact that in 1942 – 1943, the British suggested «the creation of an independent state of Transylvania on the model of the Swiss cantons»[1], whereas the British delegation had been the one which insisted, in 1944, according to the saying of Lucrețiu Pătrășcanu, on the introduction in the text of the armistice, of the formulation «Transylvania or most of it». Such a point of view was not characteristic only for the British diplomacy, but also had important supporters across the Atlantic Ocean, more precisely in the instances charged with the preparation of the documentation for the Peace Conference.

Consequently, in February 1942, there was created, about the U.S. Department of State, a Consultative Committee, put under the nominal leading of the Secretary of State, Cordell Hull, but, in reality, having as executive chairman the Sub-Secretary of State, Sumner Welles[2]. The most important structures within its framework were the Political and the Territorial Subcommittee, upon which it devolved the task to elaborate, among other things, the necessary recomandations regarding the settlement of the Transylvanian problem. Besides Isaiah Bowman, the chairman of the Territorial Subcommittee, a reputable specialist in geopolitics and international relations, among the members of these subcommittees there were: Hamilton Fish Armstrong, Adolf A. Berle, Anne O'Hare McCormick, Herbert Feis, Cavendish W. Cannon etc., assisted by many research and documentation specialists[3]. Discussed by the Territorial Subcommittee, beginning with February 1943, the problem of Transylvania has required, due to its complexity, a long series of debates. On the 5th of February 1943, the report submitted by the historian John C. Campbell, Doctor of Harvard University (1940) suggested three possibilities of solving: 1) The return to the borders of 1939, with the eventuality of a minimum modification of the frontier, solution that was considered by the reporter as the most conformable to the standards of the international law. However, this solution had the drawback of leaving one million and a half Hungarians under Romanian authority, maintaining in this way the premises of a state of conflict in that region, noticed Campbell. 2) The retrocession of the entire Transylvania to Hungary, solution considered by the reporter to be the most unfortunate of the three, because it would mean that three million Romanians would be under Hungarian domination. 3) Finally, the third solution, considered by Campbell to be the most equitable from the ethnic proportion point of view, was that of keeping the frontiers traced by the 1940 arbitration. That would be the most adequate solution to solve the problem of the Szekler territories in eastern Transylvania, alleged the reporter, but it also had a series of disadvantages that would have to be taken into consideration: the maintenance of a million Romanians and of a number of territories where the Romanians were a majority under Hungarian authority; the economic unviability of such a division; its inadequateness to the structure of the road and railway networks in the region[4]. Hamilton Fish Armstrong, one of the European problems expert from the circles near the State Department, has remarked, given these proposals, the existence of another possible solution: the one defended by Otto of Habsburg, regarding the creation of an self-governing Transylvania[5]. Despite the appreciation of this proposal by Isaiah Bowman, the chairman of the subcommittee, it was regarded with hesitation by many other members of the subcommittee; finally, it was concluded that the autonomy of this province would be possible only provided the creation of a larger Danubian confederation and the solving of the problem has been delayed for the meetings to come[6]. As for the urgent problems, with the suggestion made by Adolf Berle, it was decided that the most appropriate solution to keep under control the potentially conflictory situation in Transylvania was represented by the establishment of a direct military administration of the United Nations in this province for a period no longer than five years, until Romania and Hungary would have settled their problems and would have adopted a reasonable attitude in their mutual relations[7].

The meeting of the Territorial Subcommittee on the 12th of February 1943 has been opened, to the suggestion of the chairman Isaiah Bowman, by the discussion of the Transylvanian problem, that have been left unsettled the week before. The reviewers, Philip Morelly and John Campbell, have turned the discussion upon the problem of the Szekler territory. After emphasizing the fact that the Szeklers have always benefited by an autonomous administration, as far back as their arrival in Transylvania, preserving even after 1919 a particular cultural autonomy, Philip Mosely has considered that it would be opportune to confer autonomy to the Szekler territory, if it would be decided that it remains as part of Romania. This solution, reckoned the reporter, could be associated, for example, with a new tracing of the Romanian – Hungarian frontier, which would be preferable to a transfer of the Szekler population to the West or to its re-incorporation within the Romanian borders, without any additional guarantee[8]. Showing a special interest in the proposals suggested, Isaiah Bowman has requested the resuming of the discussions concerning the Szekler problem, in order to be adopted a just and satisfactory solution

Indeed, in the meetings of the 18th and 19th of February, the Territorial Subcommittee has declared in favour of the establishment of an autonomous self-governing in the Szekler territory, with competency in administration, education, public order etc. It has been found that the success of this experiment was connected with the observance of two essential conditions: 1) the Romanians should abandon the intention of forced assimilation of the Szeklers and should respect their rights, both as citizens of Romania and as citizens of the autonomous region; 2) the Szekler problem must not be invoked in the Hungarian revisionist campaigns[9]. This plan of creating the Szekler region's autonomy originated from the premise, emphasized the reporter John Campbell, that this territory would remain, anyway, as part of Romania. Consequently, it was considered as possible the establishment of two forms of autonomy: 1) local autonomy and regional self-governing; 2) religious and educational autonomy, including some social rights, that would be extended for the entire Hungarian population from Romania or, in other words, an attempt to determine Romania to abjure its fundamental state doctrine, with regard to the problem of nationality[10]. As part of the discussions, it has arrived to propose four projects of autonomy: 1) the reinstating of the Szeklers and the Saxons of Transylvania in their traditional privileges, associated with small territorial adjustments in favour of Hungary; 2) the autonomy of the Szekler region within the frontiers established at Trianon; 3) «the de-nationalization of Romania», meaning the protection of the ethnic minorities by a set of laws applicable to each and every citizen; 4) the transformation of the entire Transylvania in an autonomous region, as part of a tripartite state formed by Hungary, Transylvania and Romania[11].

Taking into account the opinions of its members, the Territorial Subcommittee has elaborated on the 2nd of March 1943 its proposals for solutioning the Transylvanian problem, which were forwarded to the Advisory Committee: I. After the ceasing of the hostilities, the entire territory of Transylvania – complying with the frontier existing in 1939, as an administrative line of demarcation – would remain, for a significant period of time, under the military occupation of the United Nations forces. In the meantime, there should be taken into consideration the following alternative solutions for the solving of the Transylvanian problem: 1) the return to the frontiers of 1939, fact that would maintain acute the problem of the Hungarian irredentism; 2) the ceding of the entire Transylvania to the Hungarian state, but that would mean the passing of three million Romanians under Hungarian authority; 3) maintaining the borders traced as a result of the 1940 arbitration; 4) the rectification of the frontiers of 1939 in favour of Hungary, by giving it a territory of approximately 9.000 square kilometers which would include the cities of Satu-Mare, Carei and Oradea; 5) an even more drastic rectification of the 1939 frontiers in favour of Hungary, with the object of an approximately 14.500 square kilometers territory, including most of the districts of Satu-Mare and Sălaj; 6) the creation of an autonomous or independent Transylvania in the framework of a Federation or an Union of East European or Danubian States – a solution supported by the existence of a strong provincial sense among all the nationalities; 7) the creation of an autonomous Transylvania, having special relations with Hungary and Romania – solution considered to be possible in case the two states would share a common Army and foreign policy[12].

Eventually, on the 25th of August 1943, the Advisory Committee has began to analyse the problem of Transylvania, focusing especially on the measures to be taken in the period this territory would be under the military occupation of the United Nations forces[13]. During the preliminary discussion of the problem, the Advisory Committee has reached to the conclusion that, economically, by loosing the industry existing in Banat and southern Transylvania, Romania would be a completely agrarian state, while Hungary's economy would maintain a better balance between industry and agriculture, with or without the debated region. As for the period of the military occupation, the Advisory Committee has concluded, in discussing the diverging opinions of the Territorial and Political Subcommittees, that maintaining the frontiers traced in 1940 as a line of administrative division until the final decision of the Peace Conference would represent the most simple and satisfactory solution; given this situation, the allied military governing would use the Romanian administrative personnel in the territory left to Romania and, respectively, Hungarian personnel in the territory assigned to Hungary. In exchange, the accepting of the solution which reestablished the frontiers of 1939 as a line of administrative division during the occupation would present a series of important drawbacks: this solution, involving a complete substitution of the Hungarian administrative personnel with a Romanian one, would complicate and, probably, would obstruct the actions of the military occupation authorities. The problem of the frontiers was to be resolved, too, during the occupation period, on the basis of an agreement between the victorious powers, a plebiscitary consultation of the local population being regarded as useless, practically, because of the complex ethnic distribution of this territory

Further on, the Advisory Committee has examined the seven alternative solutions suggested by the Territorial Subcommittee, formulating its own conclusions in their respect. Considered to be more or less unsatisfactory, most of them (including, among others, ceding the entire Transylvania to Hungary or maintaining the frontiers created as a result of the 1940 arbitration or, also, the return to the frontiers of 1939), the Advisory Committee has seemed to support two of the alternatives, believed to be more worthy of consideration: a) a massive frontier rectification in favour of Hungary, that included giving up most of the districts of Satu-Mare and Sălaj, altogether with an exchange of population between the two countries and the establishment of a territorial autonomy for the Szekler region; and b) creating an autonomous or independent Transylvania, as part of an East-European or Danubian Union, solution considered, however, to be feasible only in the contingency of the creation of such an union

The British – American plans regarding the organization of the peace in Eastern Europe have become completely inoperative, nevertheless, from the moment when the agreements of the three powers have attributed this area to the Soviet's sphere of domination. The Soviet diplomacy expressed earlier its interest in the Transylvanian problem. However, if in the Twenties and the beginning of the Thirties, the Soviets had affirmed the thesis about the imperialistic and multinational nature of the Romanian state and, consequently, Transylvania's right of self-determination and if they had transmitted to Budapest, later on, in the period from 1938 to 1940, numerous signs of encouragement for their revisionist aspirations, after the beginning of the war, Moscow's attitude would undergo important changes in this respect. In a note drew up by the Litvinov Commission, presented to I. V. Stalin and to Molotov, the commissary for foreign affairs, in June 1944, the following were emphasized: 1) Romania is an enemy state, that deserves a punishment, not a reward; given this situation, the allocation of Transylvania to the Romanian state can be taken into account only on the basis of some strong guarantees, which would include a close and lasting cooperation with the Soviet Union and the complete renunciation to any territorial claims regarding Bessarabia and Bukovina. Thus, by the retrieval of Transylvania, Romania would be compensated for the ceding of Bessarabia and Bukovina in the most satisfactory manner, being constrained, at the same time, to look for the support of the Soviet Union against Hungary, who would never accept as definitive its loss of Transylvania[14]. The Soviets were still taking into consideration, at the time, the alternative of forming a federation which would include both Romania and Hungary and an autonomous Transylvania, fact that would allow the Soviet Union to have a better control over the two states[15], alternative that had been abandoned afterwards, however. This way of solving the Transylvanian problem has imposed itself in Moscow, yet, long before the summer of 1944. In fact, from the very end of 1943, the right of having the first word in questions concerning the fate of Eastern Europe had been recognized, practically, to the Soviet Union by the other members of the Coalition[16]. As a consequence, the rumours regarding the Soviet intention of restoring northern Transylvania to Romania[17], without the consent of the Allies, has not left unaffected the Western political circles. On the 29th of March 1944, replying to an interpellation expressed in the House of Commons, Anthony Eden, the British minister of Foreign Affairs, affirmed that «he is not aware of the Soviet government declaration that it would retrocede to Romania the northern part of Transylvania». When a Labourist member of the Parliament, Ivor Thomas has drawn his attention to the fact that the source of this information was the Czechoslovak president, Edduard Bene□, noticing that the president seemed to be better informed than the British government in this matter, Anthony Eden has responded: «In this concern, I deal with what the Soviet government has said, not with what could have said any other person, no matter how distinguished this person may be». Ivor Thomas replied: «Should we understand from this that the British government has not received any information from the Soviet government relating to its point of view and its aspirations?». Anthony Eden's answer was: "I am not saying that. We are in permanent communication. I have only said that the Soviet government did not make such a statement»[18].

Great Britain did not have a particular policy towards Romania during the World War II. As a result of the declaration of war to Romania, made by Great Britain on the 7th of December 1941, this policy was dictated by the extensive considerations linked to the relation with its new ally, the Soviet Union. The defeat of the Axis Powers and maintaining the unity of the allies have become the most important reasons for Churchill and for Roosevelt and they have remained so during the whole war[19].

In spite of the justified cautions of the British government to let any information of this kind to reach too soon to the knowledge of the public opinion, it was already obvious that the Soviets had determined their position towards the Transylvanian problem and that it was not likely for them to be impeded by anybody to impose it. This fact has been clearly proved during the negotiations from Cairo, in April 1944, when the three Great Powers have agreed on the formulation, which was about to become the 19th article of the Armistice Convention, by which «Transylvania or most of it"was to be retroceded to Romania. The Soviet considered the Vienna Award to be an act imposed by the nazi Germany as an expression of its power and ascendancy over Eastern Europe, not as a just manner of settlement of the Romanian – Hungarian dispute[20]. Also, they took into account the fact that it would be impossible to trace a Romanian – Hungarian frontier which would be accepted as satisfactory by both sides. For this reason, the settlement of the dispute was about to become purely political and, in these circumstances, it could have been given satisfaction to Hungary only by concluding a close alliance between the Soviet Union And Hungary. At the same time, the Soviet have taken into consideration the fact that while the territorial arguments of the Soviet Union with Romania and with Finland offered these two countries a certain justification for their engagement in the eastern military campaign by the side of Germany, Hungary had entered the war without giving any justification for doing this. In return, Romania, though treated as a former enemy state, too, had a more favourable position in the Transylvanian problem. The return of northern Transylvania to the Romanian state was regarded by the Soviet as a compensation given to Bucharest for its renunciation to Bessarabia and to northern Bukovina, and, at the same time, as being strictly conditioned by Romania's attaching to the Soviet policy[21]. In case that this attachment would not have tallied with the Soviet aspirations, the Litvinov commission has drawn up an alternative plan, according to which Transylvania would become autonomous or independent as part of a federation or a confederation[22] and the Romanian – Hungarian arguments that would have come, inevitably, on this occasion, could have been easily exploited by the Soviet in order to impose their control over the region. No matter which would have been, eventually, the adopted solution, the establishment of a Soviet military administration in Transylvania was considered to be a very adequate measure; the fact that it has finally been applied only to the territory ceded to Hungary in 1940 was due, indubitably, to the great overthrow of situation from August the 23rd, 1944, that took Romania out of the line of Russia's enemies and made impossible a similar treatment for southern Transylvania

According to the explanations given by Lucreţiu Pătrăşcanu on the occasion of discussing the activity of the Romanian delegation to Moscow, the introduction of the Transylvanian problem in the Armistice Convention in the actual formulation was due to the British government, that did not want to assume any obligation concerning the European frontiers, until the Peace Conference. From the note of the United States Department of State sent to the admiral William H. Leahy, chief of Staff of the High Command of the Army and the Marine, on the 2nd of September 1944, and also from Melville's report of September the 27th 1944, military expert in the framework of the Allied Control Commission, sent to the Foreign Office by the British Legation from Bucharest, it follows that both the British and the American sides have contended that the settlement of the Transylvanian problem should be made at the Peace Conference[23]. This attitude still had well-founded military reasons, at that time. An eventual unreservedly recognition of the Romanian rights over northern Transylvania could remove Hungary's capitulation, believed the British and the Americans, and its possible rallying to the warfare against Germany[24]. This motivation given to the introduction of the 19th article has become superfluous, however, not only after the 20th of January 1945, when it was concluded the armistice between Hungary and the United Nations[25], but even from October 1944, after the removal of Horthy. From now on, the only reasons for continuing the occupation of northern Transylvania were exclusively political, being bound to the unexpressed wish of the British and the Americans to still leave certain hopes to Budapest, for the purpose of braking, if possible, the process of communisating Hungary. Nonetheless, the Soviet were already in a position to show that they disposed of an absolute power of decision, in this region, and that, from their point of view, the settlement of the Transylvanian problem could be made in only one manner: by restoring it entirely to Romania. The conditions that Romania had to accomplish, at that time, were the following: the participation of the Romanian Army's soldiers to the antifascist warfare abroad, the renunciation to Bessarabia and to northern Bukovina and, not in the last place, to bring to power a government favoured by the leaders from Moscow. Yet, in Stalin's opinion, such a government could be but one completely controlled by communists.

NOTES:

[1] Valeriu Florin Dobrinescu, «*România şi Ungaria de la Trianon la Paris (1920 – 1947). Bătălia diplomatică pentru Transilvania.*», ed. Viitorul Românesc, 1996, pp 193

[2] Ignac Romsics, « *Wartime American Plans for a New Hungary and the Paris Peace Conference, 1941 – 1947*» in «*20th Century Hungary and the Great Powers*», Edited by Ignac Romsics, Columbia University Press, New York, 1995, pp 157

[3] « *Wartime American Plans for a New Hungary. Documents from the U.S. Department of State, 1942 – 1944*», Edited with an introduction by Ignac Romsics, Columbia University Press, New York, 1992, pp 3-5

[4] *Ibidem, Document 6*, pp 117-118

[5] *Ibidem*, pp 119

[6] *Ibidem*, pp 120

[7] *Ibidem*, pp 121-125

[8] *Ibidem, Document 7*, pp 126

[9] *Ibidem, Document 8*, pp 149

[10] *Ibidem.*

[11] *Ibidem*, pp 166-167

[12] *Ibidem, Document 9*, pp 214-217

[13] *Ibidem, Document 3*, pp 232

[14] Valeriu Florin Dobrescu, *op. cit.*, pp 196

[15] *Ibidem.*

[16] Romsics, «*20th century...*», pp 164

[17] *«România Regală şi Transilvania, 1944 – 1947»*, an interview with the former king of Romania, Mihai I (the 9th of December 1993), realized by Mihaly Fulop, in *« Transilvania văzută în publicistica istorică maghiară. Momente din istoria Transilvaniei apărute în revista <<Historia>>»*, ed. Pro-Print, Miercurea Ciuc, 1999, pp 360

[18] The Archives of the Ministry of Foreign Affairs, Dos. Transilvania / 1944 – 1945, vol 139, C.A.C.

[19] Dennis Deletant *« British Policy Towards Romania: 23 August 1944 – March 1945»*, in « *6 Martie 1945. Începuturile comunizării României*», ed. Enciclopedică, Bucharest, 1995, pp 102; see also Vasile Puşcaş «*Al doilea război mondial, Transilvania şi aranjamentele europene (1940 – 1944)*», The Center for Transylvanian Studies, Fundaţia Culturală Română, Cluj-Napoca, 1995

[20] Mihaly Fülöp, «*L' occupation sovietique*», in «Relations internationales», no. 79, 1994, pp 336

[21] Virgil Ţârău, «*Problema Transilvaniei în ecuaţia comunizării României*», în «*Sovietizarea Nord-Vestului României (1944 – 1950)*», ed. Muzeului Sătmărean, Satu-Mare, pp 88

[22] M. Fülöp, *op. cit.*, pp 338

[23] Ion Şuţa, «*România la cumpăna istoriei. August '44*", ed. Ştiinţifică, Bucharest, 1991, pp 294

[24] V. F. Dobrinescu, *op. cit.*, pp 200

[25] *Ibidem.*

CHAPTER THREE

NORTHERN TRANSYLVANIA UNDER ROMANIAN ADMINISTRATION (SEPTEMBER – NOVEMBER 1944)

From the military operations point of view, a few days after the Proclamation of the King from the evening of the 23rd of August 1944, the Romanian Army has joined the Soviet forces in the antifascist war and, during September and October, it has liberated the Transylvanian districts ceded in August 1940. In September 1944, Iuliu Maniu has proposed the establishing of a Commissariat of the Romanian government for the northern Transylvania territories, structure invested with large powers. The project concerning the organization of the General Commissariat for the administration of the liberated regions of Transylvania, examined in the government meeting on the 22nd of September 1944, granted the Commissariat a competence similar to a provisional regional government, including the right to issue local authority decrees. Because Lucreţiu Pătrăşcanu (minister in the General Constantin Sănătescu's government, at the time) has required that the measures which might encourage the regionalist tendencies should be avoided and also, that the principle of the government's direct control over the entire territory of the country should be maintained, it was decided that the project is to be modified[1]. A few weeks later, on the 10th of October 1944, the King has promulgated the law no. 487, by means of which it was established the Romanian Commissariat for the Administration of the Liberated Regions of Transylvania, commissariat that was supposed to represent the authority of the Romanian government in this territory[2]. At the head of this institution has been appointed a «High Commissary» – dr. Ionel Pop – who could take any measure he considered to be necessary, in the name of the Romanian government and within the limits of the legislative framework into effect, in order to reestablish and consolidate the Romanian administration[3].

The reserve brigadier General Vasile Barbu has been appointed general secretary of the Commissariat. In addition to the Commissariat, an advisory committee has been set up, with the responsability of analysing and providing suggestions for the solving of some important problems that concerned the administration of the northern part of Transylvania. The members of this committee, appointed by governmental decision, were the following: Dr. Emil Haţieganu, Dr. Petru Groza, Dr. Sabin Manuilă, Dr. Teodor Roxin, Iosif Jumanca, Dr. Silviu Pop, Valer Ghircoiaşiu and Dr. Simon Nemeş[4] . The Commissariat was supposed to draw up decree-law and decree projects meant to reintegrate this region within the Romanian administrative system and to remove the consequences of the Hungarian legislation. Thus, among the first decree-law projects drawn up and presented to the government were:

– The Decree-Law for the regulation of the citizenship of the northern Transylvania inhabitants;

– The Decree-Law for the amendment of the Law of judicial organization, according to which it would be established the judicial instances in the liberated territory;

– The replacement of the land patents destroyed during the military operations;

– The extension of the Romanian legislation over the liberated Transylvania;

– The annulment of the consequences of the Hungarian ordinance 1440/1941 M.E. etc.[5]

All this time, Romania, as a whole, was in a state of disorganization and uncertainty, the Red Army being met with reserves. However, the authorities from Bucharest, at the same time with the surveillance of the military operations development in the autumn of 1944, have taken a few measures for the reinstatement in northern Transylvania. Therefore, «Monitorul Oficial» of the 13th of October 1944 published a Royal High Decree, from which we reproduce the following articles: – Art.1 – The stipulations of the Royal Decrees no.1624 from the 24th of August 1944, 1629 from the 2nd of September 1944 and 1864 from the 12th of October 1944 apply to the entire territory of Transylvania and of the others Romanian regions that have been subsequently liberated from the Hungarian occupation, prescribed by the Vienna Award; – Art.2 – All the infringements of the laws and dispositions of any kind, applied to the territory of Transylvania and of the others Romanian regions that were temporarily under foreign occupation, that render evident, through their determinated reasons, their pursued purposes or through the means used, a political aspect, even if they are termed so, are amnestied; – Art.3 – All the infringements of the law of any nature committed against the Hungarian state, its authorities and its public institutions are amnestied; – Art.4 – All the infringements of the laws and dispositions of the Hungarian state regarding the organization of the war economy, the military duties, the security measures and the obligations of any kind to the Hungarian state are amnestied; – Art.5 – The infringements from above are amnestied, whether they have remained undetected, or they are in process of research, of preliminary investigation, of judgment or they are irrevocably tried and even if the punishments are in course of execution, and if the punishments inflicted were entirely executed, the convicts are rehabilitated by right. These stipulations apply alike to the main perpetrators, to the accomplices, the supporters and the concealers, all the complementary and accessory punishments, the security measures and the disciplinary effects being extinguished, the convincts being reinstated in all their civil and political rights; – Art.6 – All those imprisoned, in one form or another, in jails, prisons or camps for any of the deeds stipulated in the present Royal Decree would be immediately liberated, ***ex officio***, under the solicitude of the respective Prosecutors and Prime Prosecutors, and, where the Romanian instances have not been established yet, their liberation would be made, ***ex officio***, under the solicitude of the Commander of the garrison from that locality; – Art.7 – The forced domicile, the police surveillance and the security measures of any kind imposed for political reasons or for the security of the Hungarian state are repealed; – Art.8 – All the deeds and the documents reffering to the questions stipulated in this Royal Decree will be closed ***ex officio***; – Art.9 – Those who participated to the rebellion of the 21st – 23rd January 1941 or those who, while commiting the infringements of the laws, had in view the realization of the Iron Guard Movement's ends are excepted from the benefits of the amnesty[6].

The same day, «Monitorul Oficial» has published another decree-law which stipulated the followings: – Art.1 – The fiscal debts of any kind resulted from direct or indirect taxes, fees and any quotas managed by the Ministry of Finance for taxable materials existing in those territories, established before the enemy occupation and charged to the inhabitants of the liberated northern Transylvania are annuled; – Art.2 – The income direct taxes, due to the budgetary year 1944/1945 for the income sources existing in the territories stipulated by the previous article, will be determined according to the provisions of the law for the settlement of the direct contributions of the revenues and to the code of fiscal procedure, beginning with the first day of the month that follows to the complete liberation of the occupied territory, with the tax quotas, stipulated by the laws mentioned above, reduced to a half; – Art.3 – The taxes determined according to the stipulations of the previous article become exigible on the 1st of January 1945. The Ministry of Finance could suspend, completely or in part, by a ministerial decision and with the approval of the central fiscal commission, in general and for one year, at the most, some categories of tax payers. The pursuit for the debits settled according to the provisions of the previous article was made by any means of foreclosure. – Art.4 – Any dispositions contrary to the present law are and remain abrogated[7].

The Ministry of Internal Affairs transmitted an official statement, by the general circular order no.26 of the 30th of October 1944, by means of which it recommended that «the convulsions that take place in varied towns and villages are to be avoided, to be elected the mayors wanted by the majority of the inhabitants, even though the government did not reinstated the electoral law of the constitutional regime's times»[8]. At the same time, the Ministry of the Internal Affairs gave written and telephonic orders during September and October according to which «the legal authorities, the General Administrative Inspectorate, the prefects and the praetors should immediately listen to the «community» and propose and appoint only the people that are, besides the legal conditions and through a thorough moral warranty, the expression of the will of the communal population's majority»[9]. According to the documents existent in the archives (Cluj, Bistriţa, Târgu-Mureş etc.), this operation should have finished by the 30th of November 1944.

In consideration of the stipulations of the 7th article of the decree-law for the establishment of a commissariat for the administration of the liberated Transylvania, concerning the reinstatement in their functions of all the officials who had legal rights on the 30th of August

1940, it has been established about the prefect's offices, according to the law no.577/1944, published in «Monitorul Oficial», no.221 of the 22nd of September 1944, a commission for examining the re-employment applications of the respective persons[10]. The chairmen of these commissions were to be, in general, the prefects, in some particular situations, however, being possible to option for sub-prefects, too. Among the members of the commissions were to be appointed representatives of the Romanian religions, the chiefs of the local police, the commander of the gendarmerie legion in that territory etc. It was announced, by a circular order of the Ministry of Internal Affairs (no. 9046 of the 14th of October 1944) for the occupation of the vacant positions, that the prime-praetors, the praetors and the notaries evacuated from the former administration of Bessarabia and Bukovina can be appointed in those positions[11]. In view of these, on the 19th of October, «Monitorul Oficial» has published the following decree-law: «- Art.I – The officials sent on duty in Moldavia, southern Bukovina and northern Transylvania will get a special indemnity for installation, equal to a budgetary wage, including the indemnity for high prices, except for the indemnities stipulated by the article 105 from the Code of the public functionaries; – Art.II – The special indemnity stipulated in the previous article will be given as an advance from the portofolio, being passed for payment afterwards from extraordinary budgetary credits that will be opened with that purpose in view»[12].

This measure was meant to offer decent livelihood to refugee civil functionaries, ensuring their reinstatement in the administrative system. Soon after, however, it has given rise to predictable reactions on the part of the Soviet, who pretended «the repatriation» of all the natives of Bessarabia and northern Bukovina to the Soviet Union; obviously, as for the civil functionaries, the application of this expulsion measure by the Romanian authorities would have meant, at the best, their sentence of deportation.

The reestablishment of the Romanian civil authority in northern Transylvania, despite all the problems entailed, has provoked an intense preoccupation among the academical circles, especially among the professors and the researchers of the King Ferdinand University of Cluj that have taken refuge in Sibiu during the Vienna Award. The members of the University of Cluj have promoted views according to

which the reestablishment of the Romanian legislation in the liberated territory was an indefeasible right of the Romanian state, «which had the right to decide and to prescribe, conformable to the international juridical standards and by virtue of expanding its sovereignty, any juristic norm deemed to be right and the state mechanism that it wants to organize for reaching its purposes. Also, the state is free to decide to what extent does it mean to recognize the juridical effects of the actions committed and of the rights acquired in the previous period of time, by virtue of a legislation abrogated by the reinstatement of the other one»[13].
An important problem was the manner the Romanian legislation was to be reestablished in the liberated territory. Whether the derogation of the foreign laws was to be made once for all or gradually, it is certain that a formulation like «the following laws...» or, specifying, «those Hungarian laws established during 1940-1944 are repealed and replaced by the corresponding Romanian laws» would not be satisfactory. Such a provision, lapidary and very convenient, would give rise to numerous doubts regarding the possibility of applying the legal standards and especially the future of the juridical condition supervened in the meantime. As a result, it was recommended as the only allowable method the examination of every standard, separately or in groups, if possible and, at the same time, finding solutions for the settlement of some situations existent by virtue of the Hungarian legal standards[14].
The reinstatement of the Romanian organization: administrative (of state, of district, of commune), financial, judicial, of education, industrial and commercial, of health assistance supposed a previous settlement of the public functionaries problem, because this reinstatement would be illusory, in part, if the state does not have, in reality, at its disposal qualified persons for the pursuit and the achievement of this task. One of the first questions that were asked is whether the Romanian state has the right to dismiss conjointly those people that formed until recently the structures of public services in northern Transylvania or whether, on the contrary, the former Hungarian functionaries have obtained any right to maintain their positions, obviously, to the extent of their compliance to the new exigences prescribed by an organization framework established by the Romanian state. That dilemma had to be analysed right from the start, as it was possible that claims of this kind could be formulated on both the part of the functionary corps and of some external elements. It has arrived at the conclusion that the position

of public servant has its source and its juridical legitimacy in the sovereignty of the state which confered this quality by appointement or by election. As a result, the moment this sovereignty ceases, the position of public functionary would not have any justification to persist in the lost territories. The Romanian state was considered free to maintain elements of the previous administrative structure, for reasons of opportunity, equity, charity etc., but he had no legal obligation to do so, no matter if the Hungarian functionary would have complied or not with the conditions prescribed by the Romanian state to its own functionaries: titles, loyalty oath, a thorough command of the Romanian language etc. Therefore, the functionary of northern Transylvania (who has acted beginning with the Autumn of 1940) had obtained certain rights from the Hungarian state, but not from Romania, as long as a surrender of territory does not imply, under any circumstances, any right of the functionary from the ceded territory to maintain its position in the administration of the liberating state. Thus, the Romanian state should not have felt obliged to keep in their positions the former functionaries from the liberated territories, by any of the Public Law juridical standards[15]. The reinstatement of the Romanian juridical organization will involve the establishment of a new bar of lawyers and the returning of the notaries in the positions they had previously occupied. In case that, from various reasons, the completion of the existent positions could not be made on these basis, it was allowed to make other appointments. Also, the reinstatement of the procedure legislation required a series of special provisional stipulations in order to settle the affairs in progress[16].

Right after the ceasing of the military operations, there have been taken measures, in the liberated territories, for removing the consequences of the Hungarian administration. In the beginning of November 1944, it has passed to a new administrative division of some districts of Transylvania (the territorial division of the districts of Bihor, Ciuc, Cluj, Maramureş, Mureş, Năsăud, Odorhei, Sălaj, Satu-Mare, Someş, Târnava-Mare, Târnava-Mică si Trei-Scaune are those existing on the 30th of August 1940, having the same district capitals and towns; – the district of Cluj-Turda has been called Turda, with the capital in Turda; – the territorial divisions of the district of Braşov, Câmpulung and Turda are those existing on the 30th of August 1940; – the town of

Beiuş, the provisional capital of the district of Bihor has become a non-capital town, belonging to the same district)[17] and the reorganization of the administative sectors in the main cities of northern Transylvania. Thus, we mention for exemplification the decision of the Cityhall of Cluj of the 7th of November 1944, according to which it was established in every division of the city an administrative sector instead of three sectors as it has been in the previous regime. The centers of the sectors were the following: the Circumscription I – in Unirii Square, no.2; the Circumscription II – St. Oăşanu, no.29; the Circumscription III – Victoriei Avenue, no.12; the Circumscription IV – Regele Ferdinand Avenue, no.42, the Circumscription V – St. Fântânele, no.37; the Circumscription VI (Mănăştur), with its temporary center in the building of the first circumscription, but the definitive center was to be established in Mănăştur[18]. The administrative sectors were charged with the issuing of the communal certificates, of the pauperage certificates and with the inventory of the inheritances. The competence of the sectors has extended by the fact that, beggining with that day, they will apply the orders given by the Cityhall; for instance, they would control the accomplishment of the orders concerning the public tidiness.

As for the problem of the houses, the administrative sectors have been given important powers. Since the publishing of that decision, the registering of the requests for the assignment of a house was to be made not at the Houses Office, but at the administrative sectors. «The house tickets» and the other decisions of the Houses Office were to be issued by the administrative sectors, within a week from the registration. Those who did not have a home when they submitted the request were to present themselves at the Houses Office the following day for receiving a quartering ticket with which they could live in a temporary home, until the final settlement of the request. In addition to that, every administrative sector was to organize the circumscription council, formed by the street representatives. By doing this, the inhabitants of the city were to reach direct contact with the administrative mechanism, providing a fast and successfully execution of the orders given by the Cityhall[19].

The same day, the 8th of November, the Cityhall of Cluj changed the following street and square denominations: Matyas Kiraly Square was called Libertăţii Square; Hitler Square – Malinovsky Square; Mussolini Avenue – Moţilor Avenue; St. Gombos Gyula – St. Rakosi Matyas; Szeptember II Avenue – Tudor Vladimirescu Avenue; St. Wesselenyi Miklos – St. Dozsa Gyorgy; St. Vasvary Pal – St. Josza Bela; St. Csaky Istvan – St. Moricz Zsigmond; Horthy Miklos Avenue – St. Horea; St. Tisza Istvan – St. Crişan; St. Banffy – St. Cloşca; St. Honved – St. Budai Nagy Antal; St. Apponyi – St. Tancsics Mihaly[20]. Also, it was requested that a commission would examin all the square and street names and make proposals for «the changing of the denominations of fascist and reactionary characteristics»[21]. The owners of each house or, in their absence, the house curators or the tenants were compelled to remove from the buildings the plates with the street name that was to be change and to replace them with the new names. Until the Cityhall technical service made the new plates, those who inhabited the buildings had to place on their houses cardboard or tin plates with the street's new name written on it[22].

For the proper administration of each district, it has been constituted a provisional district commission, under the leadership of the prefects. Taking into account the particular condition existent in the territory, which was the scene for the development of some devastating military operations only a few days before, by the end of October and the beginning of November, the mayors have adopted, assisted by these commissions, a series of measures for the helping and the protection of the population. Thus, in many cities, there have been created people's canteens for the following sorts of inhabitants: 1 – for the children younger than 14, whose parents did not have an adequate source of income or one from which they were not be able to support them; 2 – the people older than 55, that did not have any source of income; 3 – all those whose work disablements exceeded 50 percent and could prove that thing by a medical certificate; 4 – the mothers having at least two children under 14, whose husbands were not present and who did not have any personal source of income and their eventual earnings could not support their families; 5 – the pregnant mothers and those with baby at the breast[23].

The population entitled to the above assistance was requested to take the meal tickets from the offices of the social protection services that were opened in the main cities, bringing also the documents certifying the entitlement. At the same time, those whose rights of benefit by the people's canteen have ceased were put on guard on the compulsoriness to announce the social protection services, voluntarily and on his own responsability. Any abuse or trespassing entailed «the most serious consequences, the more so as the supply is burdened by the unfavourable circumstances, any attempt to usurp the rights of the ones lacking the means of subsistence being considered to be among the most serious guilts»[24]. There were given dispositions to suspend any activities of selling or buying houses, there were established special shop timetables and, for the purpose of defending the citizens property and security, the villages were requested to organize the communal guard[25].

The organization «Apărarea patriotică – Regiunea Cluj» (***The patriotic defense – Cluj region***) was going to adopt the same purposes, according to the declarations of its founders on the occasion of the constitution meeting, and will concern with the help of the war victims, of the families of those mobilized, of the sick, of the disasters victims and of other persons in need. The association has set up a free of charge ambulance station and a canteen, too[26]. These activities of the association were really welcome by an important part of the population but behind these charity acts has stood the propaganda of the leftist organizations which could be easily discerned from the slogans the leaders of this association have presented: «we fight for the spreading of the democratic ideas», «we fight for achieving the soldering between the front and the rear of the front», «we fight for the glory of those that have fallen in the battle, for country and democracy», «we propose ourselves to defend all true patriots and their families, that have suffered because of their democratic attitude» etc.

The Romanian authorities have payed a special attention to the instatement of the gendarmerie units in the recently liberated territories. Thus, as far back as the middle of September 1944, there were given orders for the organization and the function of the gendarmerie in northern Transylvania[27], the main concerns of which should have been: the cover of the occupied territory, from a police point of view; the quartering in good conditions of the sub-units; the supply of the sub-units with food, fodder and fuel; to take measures so that nobody would obstruct the public authorities to apply rigorously the laws and the orders in effect; to take measures for ensuring the safety of the transportation; to organize civil guards, with the help of whom would be ensured the watch of the towns day and night; to require the population to work for repairing the roads and the bridges etc.[28]

On the 10th of September 1944, through the telephone order of the General Inspectorate of the Gendarmerie no.1591, all the non-commissioned officers and the troops that formed the gendarmerie legions from northern Transylvania prior to the ceding of the territories were asked to present at the meeting centers mentioned in the respective telephone note within 12 hours, for being restored. At the same time, the non-commissioned officers and the troops subordinated to the Gendarmerie Inspectorate of Cluj in 1940 were called to present themselves in Alba Iulia, in order to undertake the archive, preserved in the meantime at the headquarters of that inspectorate[29].

Simultaneously with the beginning of the offensive for the liberation of northern Transylvanian territories, the Romanian Gendarmerie has reestablished its inspectorates, legions, stations and its posts existing prior to the dictate. Until the complete liberation of the territory, the gendarmes legions have formed police companies, that provided the battle-front police, in the meantime passing to the activities specific to the gendarmes stations and posts. By decision of the Ministry of Internal Affairs no.17838, published in the General Circular Order no.25 of the General Inspectorate of the Gendarmerie, the Gendarmes Inspectorate of Cluj resumed its activity beginning with the 1st of November 1944, in the structure of which the following legions were parts: Cluj, Alba, Turda, Someş and Năsăud[30].

The efforts of the government from Bucharest to enclose northern Transylvania inside the borders of the Romanian state have struck against a series of difficulties, the large majority of which were caused by the Soviets, who would not allow the Romanian civil servants to exert their prerogatives.

Thus, through a note sent to Marshal Malinovsky on the 10th of November 1944 by the Chief of the High Headqurters, General Nicolae Rădescu (confirmed by the Chief of the Military Convention Bureau, lt. col. Nicolae Drăgănescu), it has been pointed out to the Soviet authorities that until the 31st of October 1944, the Soviet commander of the Cluj region did not allow the installation of any civil or military Romanian authority in Cluj and in Oradea, motivating that he did not get any order, and we must specify that the order should have been given, in fact, by Malinovsky itself. Rădescu declared: «In view of the fruitful colaboration between the Soviet and the Romanian forces in the common fight of the battle-front, under your high command, and also of the fact that the front is nowadays at a distance from those cities much greater than the 100 kilometers distance stipulated by the 17th article of the Armistice Convention, I ask Your Excellency with honour to be willing to aprove and to give dispositions so that the reestablishment of the Romanian civil authorities in Cluj and in Oradea Mare would be made unhamperedly»[31]. Immediately after the note sent to Malinovsky, the Romanian civil administration has instated in these regions, too, but only for a few days.

This sort of problems has existed also in the districts where the Romanian administration succeeded to instate for quite a long time. For instance,according to a report of the district prefect, Dr. I. Bozgod, sent on the 27th of October 1944 to the High Commissary for the administration of the liberated northern Transylvanian territories, in the district of Mureş, where the Romanian administration have been established on the 16th of October 1944, the situation was pretty precarious and the findings that ensue from this report can be summarized as follows:

1) The installation of the authorities:

– since the liberation of the district, save for small exceptions, the functionaries of the various departments have not reported to their jobs in order to get in the exercise of their duties. The representatives of the Ministries of Justice, of Labour, of Health and Social Protection, of the Public Works , of Industry and Trade, of National Education (with the exception of a few elementary and secondary school principals), of Agriculture and the domains (together with every belonging branch – agricultural, zootechnic and sanitary-veterinary, sylviculture), with the exception of the director of the Chamber of Agriculture did not arrived.

2) The administrative functionaries

a) *The district prefect's office* – of the total of 34 civil servants appointed by the Ministry of Internal Affairs, there have reported by the above specified date only 23 of them, among which there were 6 janitors and two overseers. The duty was performed by the persons that have reported to their jobs, then by the former functionaries of Romanian ethnic origin, that have stayed in northern Transylvania, and by keeping a few Hungarian functionaries. The technical and the maintenance staff from the district technical service, the district attorney and the personnel specialized in registering and archive keeping were missing.

b) *The Cityhall of Târgu-Mureş* – of the 83 appointed functionaries, 50 have reported to their jobs, among which there were 8 janitors. Beside the present functionaries, the duty was provided by Hungarians, specially convoked for these positions (usually from the ones that have worked in administration prior to August 1940, but also after that date). The municipal advocate was also missing.

c) *The State administrative functionaries* – of the 11 praetors appointed to the prefect's office, 10 praetors have reported and they have been appointed in the 10 divisions of the district. Their field activity was hindered by the lack of means of transportation (the praetor's offices did not even have a cart) and by the lack of telephone connections. Of the 51 appointed notaries, a number of 39 have reported to their jobs and another 6 notaries have come from the villages that were allocated to the district of Cluj – Turda during the surrender of northern Transylvania.

d) *The functionaries from the villages* – of the 18 appointed functionaries, there have reported 9. For the carrying on of the administrative activity at all, there were hired persons who could prove that they have graduated at least the elementary school.

3) The condition of the local administration

– with the exception of the prefect's office and of the Cityhall of Târgu-Mureş, almost all the buildings of the district's townhalls have been deteriorated because of the fights that took place in the district. In the same condition were the other public or private edifices. The waterworks and the power stations in Târgu-Mureş have been destroyed by the German and Hungarian troops during their retreat towards West. The Mureş dam has also been destroyed, the city of Târgu-Mureş and the surrounding villages lacking the drinking water and the electric power for a few days. The civil status archives have been destroyed in many villages. The account books were in the same condition and the pay offices have been devastated in almost all the villages.

4) The condition of the communications

– the communication by the C.F.R. (the Romanian Railroads) was completely interrupted, it was not possible to travel by train in any direction throughout the district. The national, district and communal roads, the bridges and the footbridges were destroyed, in most cases. The special technical personnel, the engineers, the architects, the constructors etc. were missing.

5) The Law

– no court of law have started its activity, with the exception of the judge commissioned with the investigation of the possessions of the Ministry of Justice.

6) The inventory of the authorities' possessions and of the absentee individuals' possessions

– according to the facts that result from this report, by the time of its drawing up, the work of inventorying the possessions was almost finished. It has been found that, as a result of the confinement of the Jews and the leaving of the Hungarians and the Germans, their wealth, real estates, goods and chattels have passed not only in the possession of the relatives, but also to strangers or they have remained without an owner. A series of problems and incidents have resulted from the fact that the Hungarians who had taken refuge initially with the German-Hungarian troops and have been surpassed by the operative Romanian-Russian forces, as the front advanced, have returned to their localities, where they have found their homes occupied by strangers. The Romanian refugees of 1940 have come upon the same problem, when they have returned to northern Transylvania after the liberation.

7) Other necessitics

– the prefect's office has requested the authorities from Bucharest the following:

a) the immediate sending of the collection of laws, regulations and ministerial decisions beginning with 1919 to the local administrations (district, urban and rural townhalls) because all these were lacking and, by ignoring them, the executive structures could not exercise their competence;

b) the sending of all the registers and forms, especially those for the civil status, budgets, financial and administrative records;

c) the rehabilitation of the telephone lines, if not with all the communes, at least with the regional centers etc.[32]

All these problems, evoked by the prefect of the district of Mureş, did not represent a special case, because they could be found, practically, in every district of northern Transylvania, the authorities from Bucharest receiving numerous notifications in this respect.

Although in the period of time leading off with the signing of the armistice until the middle of November 1944, the statute of Transylvania seemed to the Romanians to be solved to a great extent, beginning with the advance of the Soviet-Romanian forces in the Transylvanian territory, a series of doubts and difficulties started to appear, caused by the Soviets, which did not allow the Commissariat to exercise its authority[33]. Though the liberation of Transylvania has been realized mainly by the Romanian forces, on the 25th of October 1944, when the Romanian units have finished the liberation of the country's territory and have continued the offensive over the borders, the Soviet refusal to grant to Romania effective sovereignty over this territory became more and more obvious. Of course, the Armistice Convention admitted the return of northern Transylvania (or most of it) inside the borders of the Romanian state and the 17th article explicitly recognized the right of the Romanian state to reestablish its civil administration over the entire liberated Transylvanian territory, as the armies advanced, but from the very moment of the signing of the armistice, it could have been noticed that, as for the solution adopted with respect to northern Transylvania, in the formulation of the 19th article of the Armistice Convention there was plenty of room for uncertainties. As early as October 1944, it could be frequently heard from both the Soviets and the Romanian communists the following leit motif: «Transylvania will be rendered to Romania only provided that a real democracy will be established»[34], the estimate of what it means a real or false democracy was to be made, anyway, in a totally different place than in Bucharest.

In fact, more and more alarming rumours began to reach Bucharest from the liberated Transylvanian territory, with regard to both the future of Transylvania, the relations between the local population and the Red Army soldiers and the relations between the Romanian and the Hungarian population, all these creating a state of alarm and confusion among the people. Romanian intellectuals returned from Cluj into «the free territory» accused the incomparable insolence of some Hungarian functionaries and inhabitants who refused to speak Romanian and treated the Romanians with insults. Serious conflicts have appeared when the buildings owners returned from the refuge have found their homes occupied either by Hungarians or by Soviet officers or soldiers[35].

In the big cities, especially in Cluj, there were some rumours that the taking over of the northern Transylvanian administration by the Soviet Army was imminent. On the 7th of November 1944, as a result of the rumours going about, it was already known that Moscow has appointed a commissary in the position of Governor of northern Transylvania and that this commissary already was in Cluj[36]. As a result, the frontier established by the Vienna Award was to be reinstated with Russian – Hungarian frontier guard and the returned refugees would have to go back, while those who took refuge recently with the German -Hungarian forces will be allowed to return[37]. In the districts of Someş and Năsăud there were villages where the majority of the inhabitants were Saxons. Part of the Saxons were gone, on the occasion of the retreat of the German forces from that territory, being evacuated with the German troops and part of them, being partisans, have voluntarily fled, so that in these villages there have remained only the old or ill Saxons. They told that they were not allowed by the border Hungarian authorities to go any further than the river Tisa, the Hungarians advising them to return to their native villages, because the territories they have left will return to Hungary, again[38]. These information, squeezed through various channels, have caused the Transylvanian Romanians a state of mind close to desperation.

The Romanian population has really been panic-stricken when it realized that the Romanian regiments which have fought for the liberation of northern Transylvania were sent, in totality and without exception, outside northern Transylvania. Thus, two weeks after the quartering in the village of Someşeni (district of Cluj), the 83 Infantry Regiment, which had had its headquarters prior to 1940 in Cluj, has been forced to pass the frontier of Feleac on the 8th of November 1944 and to install in the Alba Iulia garrison[39]. This circumstance has given rise, obviously, to rumours of the strangest kind. An officer of the above mentioned regiment pretended, thus, that a map of Europe has been seen, in which Romania would have had completely different borders than those from

1940 or those prior to the Vienna Award, that is the Danube mouths, Dobrudja, Maramureş, Sighet, Satu-Mare, Arad and Timişoara up to Lugoj would have a different colour, while inside Romanian colours would be comprised the Hungarian city of Debrecen[40]. In Cluj, too, on the 9th of November 1944, at about 12 o'clock, on the walls of the city has appeared an ordinance given by the prefect of Cluj, Teofil Vescan. The prefect referred in this ordinance to the order of the Military Command of Cluj, by which it was decreed the taking over of the administration of the entire territory of northern Transylvania by the Army and, in consequence, it prescribed the district's population the following: 1) – until the 12th of November inclusive, all the citizens had to enter their names on civil lists that were, at the same time, census registers of the population; 2) – all the inhabitants have been forced to declare all their belongings (animals, furniture, clothes of any sort, cereals, vegetables, lard, edible oil etc.) 3) – nobody was allowed to sell or to alienate any of their belongings, nor to draw them out of the village or the district[41]. The ordinance of the prefect also requested all the former civil servants of the Hungarian regime to resume their functions, under the threat of serious sanctions. Copies of the ordinance of the Cluj district's prefect have reached to Bucharest, through the functionaries appointed by the Romanian government for the district of Cluj immediately after the liberation, functionaries that were constrained to return, however, due to the impossibility of carying on their activity.

Keeping the functionaries of the Horthy's regime, the use of the Hungarian language and of the Hungarian state's emblems in the official papers, the will to revenge of the Romanian population for the sufferings of the 1940-1944 period, all these facts have led, in the majority of the localities with mixed population, to tension and incidents, part of which were even bloody. In this situation, the activity of the volunteers groups, formed immediately after the turning of the arms against Hungary, has gained a patriotic coloratura that many people considered to be justified.

The instructions given by the Romanian authorities, at the same time, on the 11th of September 1944, to the gendarmes units, by which it was specified that they must take action against the Hungarian Irredentism, the German population and the Iron Guard, have substantially contributed to the encouraging of the revanchist attitude of the Romanians and to the scaling of the interethnic tensions, especially in the Szekler regions[42]. The revisionism has been put abusively together with the Hitlerism, in the same category of values, attitude that was followed by the communist historiography, although revisionism did not mean, in fact, but an expression of the dissatisfactions regarding the tracing of the frontiers. That attitude is the more blamable as the problem of the frontiers was to be decided at the Peace Conference.

There was an old tradition in Transylvania that the civil defense would be done by the mobilization of the citizens guards. That is why the volunteers which reported for being enlisted have been named «guards», as in the past. In the same manner, they have also been named «detachments». After that, the name of a politician has been added, too, that is, the name of the National-Peasant Party leader. Iuliu Maniu's name was given by Ilie Lazăr, a National-Peasant figure and then, on their way to the railway station in order to get to the battlefront, the volunteers were carrying placards with this name written on them[43]. The first calls to form volunteers detachments for Transylvania have come out on the 27th of August 1944, when appeal-leaflets have been diffused in front of the editorial office of the newspaper «Curentul» from Bucharest. It was the deed of Aurel Mărgineanu, secretary of the Transylvanian refugees association. As the leaflets spoke about Transylvanian battalions, most of those willing to enlist have reported to the editorial office of the newspaper «Ardealul» (another Romanian name for Transylvania)[44]. Thus, there have been formed the volunteers regiment «Iuliu Maniu»[45] and many other battalions, among which there were the battalions «Ip», «Trăznea» and «Beiuş»[46]. The names have not been chosen by chance! Among the people that reported for enlisting, some of them had ranks of senior officers or were well-known figures, while others did not seem to be inspired by the creed in the supreme sacrifice. Many women have reported, too, for they wanted to become nurses[47]. Most of these battalions have taken part by the side of the Romanian Army in the battles of Transylvania and they have been mentioned by citation on the battlefield[48]. Because of the fact that their discipline was frequently less than ideal, these battalions have often been a source of incidents and trespasses that took place rear the battlefront. Also, in Transylvania, in the region of Braşov, another detachment named «Iuliu Maniu» has formed, irrespective of the one in Bucharest.

There are no clear accounts of the volunteer detachments that have operated in Transylvania, because they have not been subordinated to a sole command. Separate elements of the volunteer detachments that operated alongside the Fourth Army have formed their own paramilitary groups which have succeeded to operate within the Transylvanian territory for many years[49]. «Iuliu Maniu battalion of volunteers», under the command of Gavril Olteanu, seems to be one of them and it has been formed in Braşov in the beginning of September 1944, consisting of an effective force of approximately 600 volunteers (the number of the volunteers varies; there are documents that specify 5000 – 6000 of them[50]) and on the 12th of October 1944 it has shifted on its own in the region of Sfântu-Gheorghe, having in itinerary Miercurea-Ciuc – Gheorgheni – Topliţa – Reghin and even further North, staying in the occupied territory until the 15th of November 1944. The Hungarian inhabitants of this region have complained about the crimes and the robberies committed by the volunteers, so that the Soviet officers have commanded Gavril Olteanu to leave the occupied territory[51]. On the 20th of November 1944, this detachment was quartered in sourthern Transylvania. From the inquiries that were made, it was found that there have been committed abuses and robberies in many localities and that approximately 40 Hungarian inhabitants were murdered[52].

In fact, during the turmoil that followed the 23rd of August 1944, when the echoes of the atrocities perpetrated by the Hungarians against the Romanians between 1940 and 1944 began to reverberate their effects, being amplified also by the recent bloody actions that happened in the Autumn of 1944, there were detachment commanders that thought they were «called to do justice». That action can be explained, psychologically, but it cannot be excused[53]. These actions and the people who have joined these formations as well, with the intention of robbing or vengeance, have compromised the idea of fighting of the northern Transylvanian volunteers. Such things were possible because of the attitude of a part of the Romanian military commanders, that have given tasks incompatible with the dignity of the military uniform in charge of these detachments.

To this state of affairs has added the fact that northern Transylvania, and especially the region of Cluj, has started to become, right after the liberation, the scene of intense political confrontations, which would thus double the ethnic confrontations and the social and economic problems. From a political point of view, first and foremost was the National-Peasant Party, this state of things being favoured by a series of objective and subjective circumstances. On one hand, it was the obvious weakening of the part of the National-Liberal Party, the leadership of which was not rising anymore to the level of the «Brătienist decade», being affected, at the same time, by the political compromising of Gheorghe Tătărescu's group. On the other hand, there had to be taken into account the popularity of Maniu, who was hostile to the Soviets. Thus, the popularity of the National Peasant Party and especially that of its leader has succeeded to grow permanently, representing, until its interdiction, the main element of the democratical opposition in Romania[54].

The rivalry with the extreme left has been very sharp, from the very beginning. The Regional Committee of the Romanian Communist Party organized its center in Cluj right after the liberation, the authority of which has comprised Transylvania entirely. Gradually, as the Soviet forces advanced in Transylvania, it has been ascertained an intense extension of the communist net. It has come, thus, that in every district capital would function a municipal organization, the structures of which were meant to control the entire public life, and, at the same time, organizations in every rural division[55]. The main task of each district committee was to enlist in a very short period of time as many members as possible, irrespective of their ethnic origin or their political past[56]. The adhering of a large number of Hungarians to the Romanian Communist Party has created in the region acute manifestations of hostility on the part of the Romanians. Simultaneously with the propagandistic actions of the Romanian Communist Party, The Ploughmen's Front developed, in his turn, an intense campaign in the country-side, where its actions were favoured by the tacit support of the military authorities and by the fact that, yet, it was not completely identified by the people with the communists. On the 10th of November 1944, bishop Nicolae Colan draw the attention to the fact that, after he has left for two months his residence, when he returned, «he has found the Chancellery and the Diocese to be scattered by the epidemic of petty politics, while the assessor Laurenţiu Curea, president of the Ploughmen's Front in Cluj, is activating day and night in this direction, not only in the city of Cluj, but also in the entire district»[57].

All those things have taken place in a very complex conjuncture, with tones that seemed more and more sombre when the military developments, the lacks of all sorts, the abuses of the Soviet soldiers and the alarming rumours have deeply troubled the northern Transylvanian inhabitants. The documents existing in the archives evoke the state of mind of the population and testify for the things asserted. It was also found that, while right after the cease of the military operations, the Romanian refugees of the Vienna Award period have begun to return to their homes, after the 5th and the 6th of November 1944, many of them have returned to the free territories, worried about the situation they have found there.

Thus, a few weeks after the accomplishment of the liberation of northern Transylvania – liberation accomplished as a result of military confrontations in which the Romanian army has taken part with enthusiasm, its military successes being payed with a heavy tribute of casualties – it became obvious that the hopes of those who had thought that the uncertainties regarding the territory ceded on the 30th of August 1940 are over would undergo a tragic disappointment.

NOTES:

[1] «*România, marele sacrificat al celui de-al doilea război mondial...*», pp 496

[2] *Ibidem*, pp 498

[3] Ion Silviu Nistor, *op. cit.*

[4] «*Tribuna Ardealului*», the 5th year, no. 1155, the 31st of October 1944, pp 1

[5] «*Universul*», the 61st year, no. 310, the 15th of November 1944, pp 3

[6] *Idem*, the 20th of October 1944, pp 6

[7] *Ibidem.*

[8] The Romanian National Archives – Oradea (A.N.R.O.), Fund «*Inspectoratul de jandarmi Oradea*», Dossier 2/1944-1945

[9] *Ibidem.*

[10] The Central National Archives Târgu-Mureş (A.N.C.Tg-Ms), Fund «*Prefectura Judeţului Mureş, Serviciul Administrativ*», Dossier 228/1944

[11] *Ibidem*, D. 211/1944

[12] «*Universul*», the 20th of October1944, pp 2

[13] Camil Negre, «*Le probleme du retablissement de la Legislation Roumaine en Transylvanie du Nord*», The Center for Studies and Research regarding Transylvania, Sibiu, 1945, pp 25

[14] *Ibidem*, pp 26

[15] *Ibidem*, pp 26-27

[16] *Ibidem*, pp 28

[17] «*Universul*», the 3rd of November 1944, pp 3

[18] «*Tribuna Ardealului*», the 8th of November 1944, pp 3

[19] *Ibidem.*

[20] *Ibidem.*

[21] *Ibidem.*

[22] *Ibidem.*

[23] *Idem*, the 1st of November 1944, pp 4

[24] *Ibidem.*

[25] The Romanian National Archives Bistriţa (A.N.R.B-ţa), Fund «*Poliţia de Reşedinţă Bistriţa*», Dossier 4/1945

[26] *Ibidem.*

[27] The National Central Historical Archives (A.N.I.C.), Fund «*Inspectoratul general al Jandarmeriei. Direcţia Siguranţei şi Ordinii Publice*», Dossier 2/ 1944-1945, «To all gendarmerie formations from northern Transylvania, including the posts. Instructions, no.44158 from the 11th of September 1944

For the organization and the function of the Gendarmerie in Northern Transylvania (retrieved territory)

I – **Generalities:**

- the gendarmerie occupies and organizes the reconquered territory of northern Transylvania, from a police point of view, according to the present instructions, to the duty statutes in force and to the dispositions given by the United Nations operative in the area;

- the gendarmerie formations (legions, stations and posts) install normally in the territory in the former territorial circumscriptions, evacuated in 1940 and with regard to the local operative situation;
- as a rule, the distance between the battle formations on the battle line and the gendarmerie units (posts, stations, legions) which occupy the territory as a police would be that of one day of march;
- the progress of the territorial gendarmerie will be made in any case according to the local operative situation and taking into account the fact that the sooner the gendarmes enter in their positions the easier to control would be the situation and the quicker would be achieved the pacification of the area;
- with that end in view, the legion commanders will maintain a permanent contact with the United Nations Commands in the area, with which they would establish, by mutual agreement, the standards for the shifting and the installation of the territorial gendarmerie formations.

II – The organization of the service and the application of the police measures

- the legions, the stations and the posts, immediately after the installation (if possible, in their former buildings) and the occupation of the territory devolving upon them, will pass to the organization of the service according to the stipulations of the Gendarmerie Regulations;

1) – The internal organization of the unit:

a) The Legions:

- the offices will be formed and integrated conformable to the existing norms in force;
- there will be set up the necessary registers and forms (in order of the main needs);
- it will be established the contact with the superior units, of colaboration and subordination (by phone, by telegraph, by messengers, by automobile or motorcycle, by waggon, on foot etc.)
- a service of residence alarming, guard and security will be created, which would intervene in case that enemy partisans groups would pass on to violence or terrorist activities etc.

b) The stations and the posts:

- there will be set up the necessary registers and forms (in order of the main needs);
- a service of alarming, guard and security of the post's building will be created, with the aid of the local Romanian inhabitants, reliable persons, that have suffered during the Hungarian occupation;

- it will proceed to the organization of the service from a police point of view, according to the Gendarmerie Regulations.

2) – The application of the police measures

- the reinstatement of the public order and the arresting of all those who have taken to robbery, riots, destructions etc.
- the immediate organization of the information service, with the aid of the reliable Romanians in the area and it will be taken measures for the identification, the arresting and the confinement in specially intended places of all the persons that have persecuted, under the Hungarian occupation, the Romanian population in one form or another, of all the leaders or the active members of the German organizations and of the iron-guardists known as leaders or agitators;
- the preservation of the warehouses of any kind left by the enemy and the ensuring of their guard by reliable people (Romanians) from the area. The buildings where are deposited all sorts of things left by the enemy or by the Germans are to be sealed and guarded until the arrival of the authorities with competence, charged to inventory and to put them under the state patrimony;
- the closing of all Hungarian or German propaganda houses and clubs and their sealing;
- to be gathered evidences of any kind (on the spot) by which it would be ascertained the destructions, the robbery, the atrocities committed against the Romanians and any other actions of disorder. There will be taken photos as much as possible and there will be required authentic certificates to the forensic experts for all the tortures, crimes and atrocities caused to the Romanian population...;
- the identification and the arresting of all those who print, write or multiply in any manner, or distribute leaflets, sketches, drawings that would contain instigations to commit the actions which represent a plot against the order and security;
- the surveillance and the regulation of the traffic on the public roads and streets and the identification of those who create problems;
- the surveillance of the public places (taverns, cafés, hotels, inns etc.) for the pursuit and the catch of the spies, through the control and the identification of all suspect persons...;
- the control of the phone and telegraph wires, so that they wouldn't be connected to isolated locations, hidden at individuals, in houses, bushes, pits, mines etc...
- the gathering of the deserters and their sending to their units.

III – The pursuit of the security problems existing in the territory

- the security problems to be pursue are the following: The Iron Guard; The Hungarian Iredentism; the meetings of the German population; the espionage, the terrorism, the paratroopers; the alarmism and the defeatism; the instigations to rebellion; the strikes and the sabotage; the tresspassing of the frontiers and the incidents on the frontier; the population's state of mind, in general (with reference to the Romanian rural population, the minoritary population and the foreign citizens, various citizens of a special condition for the state mechanism, the orphans, the widows and the war disabled, the merchants and the industrialists, the artisans, the workers, the refugees and the floating persons); the press and the mail;
- the state of mind inside the gendarmerie;
- the following will not represent security problems and, as a result, they will not be surveyed any longer: socialism, communism and the Ukrainian Irredentism...»

[28] A.N.R.O., Fund «*Inspectoratul General al Jandarmeriei Oradea*», Dossier 2/1944-1945; A.N.R.B-ta, Fund «*Legiunea de Jandarmi a Județului Năsăud*», Dossier 1/1944-1945; A.N.R.Tg-Ms, Fund «*Prefectura Județului Mureș*», Dossier1/1944

[29] Cornel Oprean, Corneliu Nuț, Ion Pobirci, «*Jandarmeria Ardeleană – tradiție și contemporaneitate*», ed. Dacia, 1999, pp 100

[30] *Ibidem*, pp 100-101

[31] Archives M.A.E.S.A., Fund 71/1939 E9, year 1944-1947, vol.189

[32] A.N.R.Tg-Ms, *Fund cit.*, Dossier 1/1944

[33] Claudiu Porumbăceanu, «*Situation administrative et politique du departement de Satu-Mare du 25 octobre au mois de mars 1945*», in «Transylvanian Review», vol.IV, no.4, Winter 1995, pp 86

[34] Victor Frunză, «*Istoria stalinismului în România*», ed.Humanitas, Bucharest, 1990, page 165

[35] A.N.R. Cluj, Fund «*Biroul de Cenzura Cluj-Turda*», Dossier 9/1944-1945

[36] *Ibidem.*

[37] *Ibidem.*

[38] *Ibidem.*

[39] *Ibidem.*

[40] *Ibidem.*

[41] *Ibidem.*

[42] «...For the pursuit of the problems that are taken into account, it is drawn the attention especially to the actions to be carried on against the Hungarian Irredentism, the German population and the Iron Guard. These problems are to be pursued at full intensity, knowing the fact that the Hungarian chauvinists and also the Germans grouped in Hitlerite formations and the iron-guardists left in the territory at the time of the ceding or refugees from the country, are elements that will never be able to integrate with the order structure of the Romanian state. All those identified to be activating in any manner will be immediately arrested and forwarded to the Courts Martial...», A.N.I.C., Fund «*Inspectoratul General al Jandarmeriei*», Dossier 2/1944-1945

[43] Gabriel □epelea, «*Însemnări de taină*», ed. Fundaţiei Culturale Române, pp 27

[44] *Ibidem.*

[45] *Ibidem.*

[46] A.N.I.C., Fund «*M.A.I.Direcţia Administraţiei de Stat*», Dossier 19/1944-1945

[47] *Ibidem.*

[48] Gabriel □epelea, *op. cit.*, pp 29

[49] A.N.I.C., *Fund cit., Dos. cit.*

[50] M.A.E., *Fund cit., Dos. cit.*

[51] A.N.I.C., *Fund cit., Dos. cit.*

[52] *Ibidem*; M.A.E., F.71/1939 Transylvania, Year 1944/1947, vol. 189

[53] Gabriel Tepelea, *op. cit.*

[54] Gheorghe Onişoru, «*Arh. totalitarismului*», year III, no.2/1998

[55] Liviu □ârâu, «*Dezvoltarea structurilor de putere ale Partidului Comunist Român în judeţul Cluj, 1945-1946*», The Year Book of the History Institute of Cluj-Napoca, XXX/1993, pp 277

[56] *Ibidem.*

[57] «*Tribuna*», new series, year III, no.41, 10th-16th of October 1991, pp7

CHAPTER FOUR

THE SOVIET ADMINISTRATION IN NORTHERN TRANSYLVANIA (NOVEMBER 1944 - MARCH 1945)

The internal political situation has changed radically in November 1944. The resignation of the Prime Minister Constantin Sănătescu has given the Kremlin and especially the local agents of the Communist Party the opportunity to hope for a rapid taking over of the power. However, the decision of the King to entrust to the same general Constantin Sănătescu the forming of new government has been a blow to the Moscow's plans, although the communists have got more portofolios in the new government than in the previous one. From that moment, Transylvania has become a really efficient means to blackmail for the Soviets, who have decided to condition the return of northern Transylvania to Romania by the accepting of a communist government by the King. So that, on pretext of some so-called security reasons and of the necessity to prevent the interethnic incidents, Stalin has decided to remove northern Transylvania from the authority of the Romanian state.

Even under the pretext of ensuring the security of the rear battlefront's area, there is no noubt that, in fact, the Kremlin wanted to have a means at its disposal to put pressure upon the Romanian government, the reestablishment of the Romanian authorities in that area becoming soon a stake in the struggle for power of the Romanian Communist Party[1].

A different administrative regime has been established, thus, initially in the districts of Cluj, Năsăud and Someş, then it has been extended over the districts of Bihor, Satu-Mare and Sălaj, too. In the districts of Ciuc, Mureş, Odorhei and Trei Scaune, where the Romanian authority had already been established, the Soviets have prescribed the withdrawal of the Romanian authorities, coming thus to the generalization of the new system by the 14th of November 1944. In fact, in the entire northern Transylvania, the Romanian prefects and mayors have functioned only in the districts of Ciuc, Mureş, Odorhei and Trei Scaune and that has happened only in the period of time between the second half of October 1944 and the 10th-14th of November the same year. In all the other districts, the representative of the Romanian administration have exercised their prerogatives only for a few days or not at all, as it has happened, for instance, in the district of Maramureş. The Soviet authority has been exercised through the agency of the recently created Executive Committee for Northern Transylvania, structure that was under Soviet control and that replaced both the commissariat proposed by Iuliu Maniu and the district committees of the Democratic National Front. The members of that Executive Committee were: Teofil T. Vescan – chairman, Jordaly Lajos – joint chairman, Teodor Bugnariu, Bruder Ferenc, Demeter Janos, Miklos Goldberger.

A report from November 1944 addressed to general Constantin Sănătescu, chairman of the Council of Ministers, is telling for the administrative and political condition in that region, resulting from that report that the Romanians authorities were not allowed to accomplish their duties and that, in many places, they were not even admitted, that the Soviets were appointing prefects and mayors, especially, and that the rejection of the Romanian authorities was due to political reasons, reasons that may be settled through the intervention of the Romanian government[2].

The withdrawal of the Romanian administration has had a negative impact both on the population and the politicians. The more so as the Soviets requested, in addition to the withdrawal of the civil authorities, the disarmament of the Romanian military units which have not been removed yet from the territory. The brutality with which the Romanian authorities were dismissed results also from a telegraphic report of the Târgu Mureş Police Inspectorate from the 11th of November 1944. On the 11th of november 1944, at 1 o'clock p.m., in a meeting presided by the leader of the Soviet Command in the city (where have taken part the prefect of the district, the commander of the gendarmes legion and the chief of the local police), he has announced that the employees from The Old Kingdom (Wallachia and Moldavia) must leave at once this part of Transylvania. The meeting ended at a quarter past one p.m. and the employees were given 30 minutes to leave their jobs[3]. In the district of Sălaj, the Fourth Army Corps, with its headquarters in Zalău, has got the order to leave the territory by the 13th of November 1944, at 6 p.m. The civil authorities, also. Because the order has not been executed within the time limit neither by the civil authorities, nor by the military authorities, witnesses of the developments related that the Soviet officers have taken the following actions: «...the district prefect has been chased away by the gun while the sub-prefect has been bound tight and removed in this way. It seems that against the Fourth Army's elements there has been made use of the weapons. The commander of the Fourth Army would have ordered to put up resistance and there were downright fights flaring up, with big losses on both sides. At the same time, this commander has sent a report on the 20th of November to the Romanian authorities from Bucharest, in which he showed that all the impediments that were opposed to the establishment of the Romanian administration in northern Transylvania, the driving away of the gendarmes, of the police, of the civil servants were made with the purpose of forcing Romania and that the people has changed its aversion to the Soviets into hatred»[4].

As a reaction to the Soviet claims, in the meeting of the Council of Ministers of the 13th of November 1944, Constantin Sănătescu has mooted the question of the administration of northern Transylvania and, despite the attempts of Petru Groza, Gheorghe Gheorghiu-Dej and Lucreţiu Pătrăşcanu to justify the Soviet action, the majority of the participants in the Council of Minister's meeting have emphasized its real reasons and also its political implications in the future[5]. General Sănătescu declared, alarmed by the brutality of that order and under the influence of the unsuccessful discussions with Malinovsky and with Vishinsky: «We are facing a precise order that does not require any discussion. We proceed immediately to its execution»[6]. Ghiţă Pop, the minister of religions and arts, considered, however, that it is impossible for Romanians to simply accept this order and to obbey what it is imposed to them. He emphasized, also, that it is necessary for Romania to define its point of view in a document which would remain valid and would be used at the peace conference that was about to come[7]. That question has also been requested by Nicolae Penescu, minister of the internal affairs, when he drew the attention upon the necessity that «the point of view of the Romanian government should be so well and clearly stated that it would not represent any longer a recognition on our part of a modification in the armistice's conditions»[8].

Given the recently created situation, during the months that followed the action of the 23rd of August until the 6th of March 1945, the two Romanian Prime Ministers, Constantin Sănătescu and Nicolae Rădescu, have repeatedly requested the removal of the administration imposed by the Soviets and the reinstatement of the representatives of the Romanian administration in northern Transylvania, without result though. On the 14th of November 1944, the Romanian government has addressed the Allied Control Commission a memorial by means of which it protested against the Soviet request. It was specified that the establishment of the Romanian administration did not contravene neither to the 17th article of the Armistice Convention (a distance of 50 – 100 km from the battlefront line) nor to the 19th article, because the very condition of the confirmation of this compulsory agreement by the Peace Treaty meant that by the treaty it would be confirmed an existing state ***de jure*** and ***de facto***, created according to the specified stipulations of the Armistice Convention. Therefore, the Romanian government was asking the Allied Control Commission «to be willing to examin and to determin, as soon as possible, the manner this reestablishment would be realized, as it is urgently required not only by the most significant interests of the Romanian state, but also by the extremely hard condition in which the population of these regions find itself»[9].

Marshal Malinovsky, replying to the Romanian government on the 20th of November 1944, stated the following: «The Armistice Convention stipulates that the question of Transylvania will be settled by the Peace Treaty, when it will also be decided if the entire Transylvania or most of it would be part of the Romanian state. Therefore, until the signing of the Peace Treaty it is not possible to reestablish the Romanian administration in Transylvania»[10].

The reactions of the leaders of the Romanian political parties have shown up immediately, also. Iuliu Maniu addressed to Vishinsky a letter on the 16th of November 1944, mentioning that, although the battle front limits have gone long beyond the 100 kilometers distance from the frontier between Transylvania and Hungary, the administration of that province has been only partly entrusted to the Romanian government[11]. The same Vishinky has also received a memorial drawn up by the leadership of the National Liberal Party, that expressed, in its turn, the dissatisfaction to the Soviet decision[12].

Acquainted on the 12th of November 1944 with the decision taken by the Soviets, the U.S. representative in Romania, Burton Y. Berry informed the American government, through a telegram addressed to the U. S. Secretary of State, C. Hull, on the withdrawal of the Romanian civil administration from Transylvania. The following were specified in the telegram: for a period of two weeks, the Romanian population was worried because of the information about the withdrawal of the Romanian civil authorities from Transylvania. The government would not allow the publishing of any document, but among the people persists the feeling that the Soviets obstruct the mending of the unjustness done to Romania by the Vienna Award. According to documents that were confidentially given to me from the Ministry of Foreign Affairs, general Vinogradov has addressed a letter on the 12th of November to the Prime Minister Sănătescu, acting on behalf of the Allied Control Commission. After reviewing the activity of the gendarmes Romanian regiment that operates in Transylvania, the general has stated in his letter essentially the following: «1) – the establishment of the Romanian administrative officials in Transylvania is forbidden; 2) – the gendarmes regiment that operates in Transylvania must be dissolved, the men shifted from Transylvania and the commander must be brought to the Court Martial and charged with instigation against the Red Army; 3) – if the request is not completely accomplished by the 17th of November, the Red Army will dissolve the regiment»[13].

The anxiety of the population given the developments in the northern Transylvanian territory has been intensely reflected both in the press of those times (especially in «Tribuna Ardealului») and in the reports drawn up by the civil and military authorities. A document existing in the archives of Cluj-Turda Board of Censors, dated the 12th of November 1944, records the charges that were brought to the authorities from Bucharest and especially to the Ministry of Internal Affairs that, according to many Transylvanian Romanians, would not know what is going on in the country. The central authorities were blamed for ignoring the reality from northern Transylvania, even more than the simple citizens do, that is, the fact that the Romanian administration has been established only in a few districts, that in some localities the authorities have been established but they were forced to leave the territory by a fixed deadline, while in others they were not even admitted»[14].

At the same time, Iuliu Maniu has addressed to Burton Berry, pointing out the Soviet Union's intentions in connection with Romania[15]. Maniu informed the American diplomat about the installation of the Hungarian communists in the administrative positions of northern Transylvania and the entering of that province under Soviet and Hungarian administration[16]. This statement was also supported by the newspaper «Dreptatea». In the article «On some statements concerning northern Transylvania and on the reality of the facts»[17] it was specified that in Bihor and in Satu-Mare, the administration has at the head former elements of the Hungarian administration, both at the district and city level, while the Romanians were taking part to the extent they were permitted to. Nonetheless, the same article specifies that in Satu-Mare the situation has changed by the end of 1944 and the beginning of the following year, through the election of a Romanian district prefect, member of the National Peasant Party.

On the 28th November 1944, Eugen Filotti has discussed with Roy Melbourne, Prime Secretary of the American Mission in Bucharest and he has been informed that the majority of the questions related to the application of the armistice have a political aspect, also. The diplomat has expressed his dissatisfaction to the Allied Control Committee's request regarding the withdrawal of the Romanian adninistration from northern Transylvania. Also, the two have raised for discussion the problems connected with the statute of Bessarabia and Bukovina, too[18]. Evoking thc war actions, the British writer Voigt noticed that «the Soviet Union has violated the Armistice Convention, keeping under direct administration not only Transylvania, but also Moldavia»[19]. In fact, the Soviet action, which has had practically the assent of the British and the Americans, also, by their actual non-involvement in preventing the removal of the Romanian administration, in addition to the fact that it represented a disloyal act towards an allied state, it reminded of the ambiguity that still hung over Transylvania.

Concomitantly with the request to disarm and retreat the regular military units, Malinovsky demanded the dissolving of the Romanian irregular troops that operated in Transylvania. Iuliu Maniu has taken the necessary steps in replying to this imperative, but his efforts were considered by the Soviet side to be tardy. In the commentary broadcasted by Moscow radio station, during the transmission of 5 o'clock on the 21st of November, there were emphasized the merits of the Red Army leaders, that would have liquidated in Transylvania «the groups of bandits, that call themselves volunteers groups, national guards etc.»[20] .

Actually, given the Soviet claims, the Romanian authorities have taken immediate action for accomplishing the orders. This fact results right from the report sent on the 14th of November 1944 to the Allied Control Commission by Ionel Pop[21] . Thus, the Romanian government has disposed that all Romanian administrative authorities existing in the Transylvanian territory, liberated by the Romanian Army and by the Red Army, would quit that territory. It has ordered the retreat from the territory and the immediate demobilization of the volunteers regiments and it has disposed that the military justice would investigate the deeds imputed to these formations. It has been drawn the attention of the Allied Control Commission to the fact that the problem of Transylvania, with its frontiers traced by the Peace Treaty of Trianon, is a vital matter for Romania and that the Armistice Convention established that northern Transylvania would enter under the Romanian state's sovereignty. However, the Romanian government, among others, has discovered the divergency that appeared by the middle of November 1944, regarding the reinstatement of the Romanian administration within the territory. And that was the more so as according to the 17th article of the convention, it was said nothing about a future or an eventual reinstatement of the Romanian civil authorities in the liberated Transylvania, on the contrary, the Romanian administrative structures were to accomplish the instructions and the orders of the Allied High Command. The Romanian civil authorities had important obligations, not only for the reestablishment of the order and security within the entire Romania's territory, but also for the fulfilment of the armistice's conditions. Nevertheless, the obligations assumed by Romania in the Armistice Convention regarded necessarily Romania as a whole, as it was impossible to carry them out without the administrative and economic support of northern Transylvania. On the grounds of that state ***de jure***, as the battlefront was moving beyond the 50 – 100 kilometers limit, the Romanian government has reinstated or has tried to reinstate the Romanian administration in the liberated territories, considering as unnecessary the conclusion of a special convention with the Allied (Soviet) High Command. The reestablishment of the Romanian civil administration in northern Transylvania has not been done clandestinely, nor by avoiding the Soviet military authorities. The Romanian authorities have come, everywhere, in immediate contact with the Soviet commanders in the region, their installation taking place in sight and with the knowledge of these officers. In some places, like in Târgu-Mureş on the 30th of October, representatives of the Soviet Military Command have been present at the small festivities organized by the Romanians[22].

Until the 16th of November 1944, there have been evacuated from the northern Transylvanian territory all the Romanian civil authorities installed there. A few teams of the Romanian Railways have remained, at the request of the Soviet military authorities, for the rehabilitation of the deteriorated railway lines and for some postal services.

The interdiction of the establishment of the Romanian civil authorities or their withdrawal from Transylvania, where it has been necessary, and the imposing of an administration subordinated to the Russian interests have meant, in fact, the maintenance of a state of insecurity, with negative consequences upon that province.

After the passing of the battlefront and especially after the removal of the Romanian civil servants, an administrative chaos has been created. Besides the fact that there were lacking a leading central authority and professional functionaries, some functionaries, during their withdrawal alongside the Hungarian – German armies, have left the townhalls in a deplorable state. The communal funds in cash, the cash registers and also the administrative registers have been stolen or destroyed. In a few localities, even the civil status registers and the communal cadastral sheets were nowhere to be found[23]. Most of the archives have been devastated and destroyed[24].

As for the persons that held positions in the administration of the region, it can be affirmed that they did not belong to a single party and that they have had the assent of the local Soviet authorities, in a large majority. By comparing the sources, a series of conclusions can be drawn. For instance, in the South and the East of Transylvania, immediately after the cease of the military operations, the local administration has been exercised by the Romanian government, by means of both Romanian and Hungarian or German persons[25]. In north-western Transylvania, in Satu-Mare, for example, from the 25th of October 1944 until the 13th of November 1944, the leadership of the district has belonged to the Hungarians, in an overwhelming proportion, while since the 13th of November, a totally different administration would establish in the district. Yet, the situation appear to be the more bizzare as we think that on the 12th of November the Soviet Command had taken over the administration of northern Transylvania and, normally, the situation should have been completely opposite, with a Hungarian communist majority after the 12th of November 1944.

Obviously, it can be asked why have the Soviets accepted a civil administration after the 12th of November 1944. We are in position to affirm that, although the Soviets have put pressure all the time upon the Romanian Commissariat and obstructed it to carry on its activity, they did not actually control that region prior to the 12th of November. Still, as they were convinced that in Romania will be established a government of the Left, shortly after the 23rd of August 1944, the Soviets have done nothing but avail of their presence in Transylvania for bringing representatives of the Communist Party to lead that territory.

As for the fact that many of the persons supported by the Red Army officers, that have held various positions in the administration, were of Hungarian nationality, the explanation is very simple. At that moment, the majority of the members or sympathizers of the Communist Party in the region were Hungarians, fact that has profoundly displeased the Romanian population of that region. As a matter of fact, the Soviet Command supervised the situation, encouraging thus the local leftist forces to take hold of the leading positions. Still, there have been two exceptions from this situation, that is the police and the political police department, over which the civil administration had no authority whatsoever, the appointments and the control of these institutions representing the privilege of the Soviet Military Command.

Right after the installation of the persons accepted by the Soviet at the head of the prefect's offices, there have been appointed the local praetors, then the notaries and the mayors of the villages, through decrees given by every prefect. Many of the persons that have been commissioned with the leading of the local administration were recruited from the ones who had held positions during the period of the Hungarian administration, also. For instance, the mayor of the city of Târgu-Mureş was a former high functionary of the Hungarian Ministry of Foreign Affairs[26]. All of them have been approved, however, by the Soviet Military Command. Also, once they were installed, the new authorities have benefited by a certain autonomy. The district's prefect had the supreme authority and a large competence by wielding entirely the prerogatives of the executive and legislative power. The public, social, administrative, economic, financial, health assistance and the urbanistic activities were managed on the basis of prefect's ordinances. The appointment of the civil servants was, also, an exclusive prerogative of the prefect[27].

During the following weeks, there were appointed officers of the Soviet Army to every prefect's office, notary's office and townhall that had the task, mainly, to supervise and to guide the application of the Armistice Convention's stipulations. Thus, through the order no.972811/1944 of the General Headquarters it was notified the fact that, according to the 18th article of the Armistice Convention, the Allied Control Commission would delegate authorized Soviet officers in the cities – district capitals, altogether with their collaborators, «having the task to apply the conditions of the Armistice within the respective district's territory»[28].

The main prerogatives of these mandatory officers were the following:

! to control and to ensure the preservation of the goods evacuated from the territory of the Soviet Union and existing at that moment in the districts (for example, materials from the endowment of some factories and plants, locomotives, freight cars, automobiles, historical monuments, works of art etc.);

! to control the organization of taking delivery of the military goods belonging to Germany and its satellites;

! to control the bringing in and the spreading of the litterature, journals and other publications, of the theatrical and cinematographic performances;

! to establish, according to the indications of the Allied Control Commission, the activity programme of the radio stations, of the postal services, of the telegraph and to perform an effective control over them[29].

Also, there has been stipulated furthermore the establishment of a commission in each district, beside the prefect's office, which was to survey the observance of the guidance received from the Allied Control Commission, in order to carry out the decisions of the Armistice Convention. The commission was formed of: the district's prefect – as chairman, and the members: the commander of the garrison, the chief of the District Economic Service, the Financial Administrator, the commander of the District Operation Center, the commander of the Territorial Circle, the mandatory of the Chamber of Commerce and Industry, the mandatory of the Chamber of Agriculture, the mandatory of the Chamber of Labour and, where there was any, the Industrial Inspector[30].

Trying to remove, as much as possible, the chaos from the administration, the Soviets have accepted on the 22nd of November 1944 the application of an order of the Ministry of Internal Affairs from Bucharest, issued on the 3rd of November 1944, in the northern Transylvanian districts, through which there were established Councils of Collaboration and People's Councils. These councils have proved to be extremely useful, as it was found that the townhalls, the praetor's offices and the prefect's offices lacked the support of the structures depending on the other ministries. For instance, the mayors did not have any information on the activity of the sanitary, agricultural, educational, ecclesiastical, veterinary structures etc., nor the latters had on the activity of the townhalls and the prefect's offices, depriving thus each other of the mutual assistance. There were not few the cases when clear contradictions appeared between the actions of these institutions[31]. In other words, there was missing a horizontal co-ordination between the administrative authorities within the framework of the same territorial unit. The members of these councils were not elected, but they were appointed on the basis of consulting the inhabitants. They had no political purpose within the administration, they could not represent the local population, the prerogatives devolving upon them were exclusively of a technical nature, aiming at the co-ordination of the local authority's actions[32].

At the same time, with a view to the welldoing of the administration in the districts with a more numerous population and in the cities, in December 1944 it was decided to reinstate the positions of General Secretaries of the cities and of the districts, secretaries that were subordinated directly to the prefects. In the district of Cluj, for instance, that position has been held by Vasile Pogăcean, the district prefect beginning with the 22nd of December 1944, as a result of Teofil Vescan's resignation[33].

There has also been instituted a «Commission for purification» around each of the prefect's offices and the townhalls, as a first sign of the times to come, upon which it devolved the prerogative, according to the ordinance no.295/1944 of the Allied Control Commission, to «suspend provisionally all those functionaries that prove to be adverse to the democratic laws»[34].

Actually, the Soviet Military Command, even from its installation, through the commanders appointed in every district, has acted as a discretionary authority, the district administrative structures getting orders from it. Warranting, first of all, every decision of the prefects, the Soviet military commander put into practice, implicitly, the orders he got from the superior hierarchical organs. In this manner, it has been started, in the beginning with a certain discretion, then without any restraints, a programme of appointing people with leftist views in the leading positions. As the activity of some mayors and prefects (for example, Teofil Vescan – the prefect of Cluj, Teodor Sbarcea – the prefect of Năsăud or that of the prefect of Satu-Mare, important member of the National Peasant Party in the region), was considered to be incongruous with the Soviet Union's interest, they have been forced to leave their positions. At the same time with the appointments of persons with leftist political views, the prefect's offices have begun to benefit by a much larger authority and autonomy – all the public, social, administrative, economic, financial, sanitary and urbanistic activities carrying on since then almost exclusively on the basis of the prefect given ordinances. The appointing of the civil servants has become one of the prefect's exclusive competences, who could remove to his liking any person from the administration, if he was considered to be a «reactionary element»[35].

Simultaneously with these actions, in Cluj there has been formed a northern Transylvanian Government, in which there were taking part representatives of some leftist organizations (the Democratic Union of the Transylvanian Romanian, the Northern Transylvania Secretariate of the Romanian Communist Party, the Social-Democrat Party, the Hungarian People's Union, the trade-unions, the Ploughmen's Front, the Patriot's Union, the Jewish Democratic People's Alliance, the Patriotic Defense). The organization has also been known as the Consultative Body of Northern Transylvania, a kind of a parliament, as it was regarded by the representatives of the Romanian population. In fact, this structure was regarded somehow differently by the Romanians and by the Hungarians, the only common fact was that they both considered it to be a creation of the Left, within which there were included representatives of various social and occupation categories and also of all the nationalities from Transylvania. For instance, in the Romanian press, especially in «Tribuna Ardealului», this parliament was accused of wanting the independence of the region and the forming of a constitution of Swiss manner. It was supposed, also, that at the Peace Conference, that structure would ask for the extension of this regime over the entire territory of Transylvania[36]. In the Hungarian press, it was thought that this Consultative body had legislative power, developing its activity through the agency of the special commissions with ministerial competence. Its main tasks were the establishment of the self-governing in northern Transylvania and the starting of the public life's democratization process, but it had also in view some measures to improve the population's everyday life, by creating canteens for the poor, supporting the people returning from the war or by taking a stand in cases of interethnic conflicts[37].

As for the public order and security, in the autumn of 1944, the General Inspectorate of **the Gendarmerie** has ordered the reinstatement of its legions in the districts of northern Transylvania, as these districts were liberated from Hungarian occupation. The Soviet military command, however, has forbidden the installation of these legions, forcing them to retreat, and the ones that were allowed to stay were forbidden to exercise their prerogatives for a longer time, compelling them to place themselves at the disposal of the General Commander of the Stages. That was the case for the Gendarmerie Legions from Satu-Mare, Sălaj and Maramureş[38]. The legions withdrawn from northern Transylvania have functioned, until their reinstallation in that territory, within the radius of other legions from the other districts of the country. For example, there have been quartered in the Gendarms Legion of Prahova most of the Trei Scaune's Gendarmerie Legion' s effectives, then they have been transferred in Valea Călugarească, an area considered to be at that time very sensitive from a police point of view. Small effectives of soldiers and officers from that legion have been detailed in the industrial areas where it was thought that paratroopers launching and sabotaging would be possible[39]. Mureş Gendarmes Legion has been initially transferred in the district of Râmnicu-Sărat and a few weeks later in the district of Putna, replacing the Ciuc Gendarmes Legion, which has been assigned a mission in the district of Bacău, in the coal region of Comăneşti[40]. In fact, beginning with the 15th of November 1944, according to the General Headquarters order no.71202/the 13th of November 1944, communicated with the order no. 33353/the 14th of November 1944 of the VI Territorial Corps' commander, the gendarmes legions from northern Transylvania retreat with their entire effective and group themselves as follows: Cluj Gendarmes Legion in the village of Luduş, district of Turda; Năsăud Gendarmes Legion in Vatra Dornei; Someş Gendarmes Legion has stayed at the disposal of the General Command of the First Army's Stages, for supplementing the guard units, shifting afterwards according to the orders of that command[41].

Later on, beginning with the 1st of December 1944 on the basis of the Instruction no.173/1944 of the General Inspectorate of the Gendarmerie, part of the gendarmes formations are dissolved, while others get new denominations, Cluj Gendarmes Inspectorate receive in its subordination Mureş Gendarmes Legion, that was transferred at that time in Târgu Ocna, district of Bacău and Târnava Mică Gendarmes Legion. On the 5th of December 1944, Someş Gendarmes Legion, after an eight day march, altogether with the 4th Sector Stage's Command, establish its headquarters in the garrison of Tăşnad, then, on the 23rd of December retreat from the Stages area and install with full effectives in the village of Mihai Viteazul, district of Turda, being at the disposal of the General Inspectorate of the Gendarmerie. As a result of operative needs, beginning with the 5th of January 1945, the same legion, with its entire effective, shift to the garrison of Sibiu, being placed at the disposal of that inspectorate, with police specific missions[42].

The beginning of January 1945 finds the Romanian Gendarmerie with the following structure: the General Inspectorate of the Gendarmerie, the General Sub-inspectorates, the control superior officers, the supplies warehouse, schools, training centers etc. On the 1st of January 1945, the Gendarmes Inspectorate of Cluj had its center in Turda, with the gendarmes formations from northern Transylvania still missing from their main bases. Beginning with the 1st of March 1945, the called-up gendarmes began to be discharged[43].

According to an order of the General Headquarters, it has been decided that the legions withdrawn from northern Transylvania would function as administratively distinct formations, depending only from a police point of view on the legions within the radius of which they were disbanded. The effectives of these legions have been used by the «host legions» in important missions of the police, in checking points, patrols etc., as it was not admitted that the Transylvanian gendarmes would be transferred to the territorial posts for supplementing the possible missings. «The host legions» had the obligation to help the legions withdrawn within their territory in the quartering and supplying operations[44].

After the withdrawal of an important number of legions, the entire northern Transylvanian territory was deprived of a serious authority commissioned to ensure the public order. Due to the fact that there was no any organized gendarmerie, the cities were studded with improvised policemen, often looking suspicious, and in the villages, there have been formed communal guards, on the model of the 1918's ones, with the purpose of maintaining the villages order and for watching, armed with weapons given by the Soviet Army[45]. These guards were formed of 8 to 10 people, generally under the command of the police station's chief, but also of the mayor or even of the Soviet mandatory, where there was any[46].

Actually, after imposing control over the public administration, the Soviets have concentrated their attention on ensuring the public order by creating police structures subordinated to their interest. Thus, by the end of November and in December 1944, the prefect's offices have issued, with the approval of the Soviets, a series of ordinances by which it was decided the setting up of the district gendarmerie. The organization standards of the district gendarmerie have been established by a special regulation. The commander of the gendarmerie that operated around the prefect's office was charged with the recruiting of the needed staff. The persons that wanted to be part of the gendarmerie had to fulfil the following conditions: 1) – to have an age from 25 to 40; 2) – to be honest citizens, untainted by common law convictions; 3) – not to be affiliated to political organizations; 4) – to speak very well Romanian and Hungarian; 5) – the ones with no domestic difficulties were preferable, so that they could be detailed in any district garrison; 6) – the recruits were to sign an written engagement by which they accepted to execute their duties in the locality decided by the Command[47]. As for the gendarme's pecuniary rights, they have been given partially both during the autumn and the winter of 1944, but they have been regulated only in January 1945 when it was decided by an ordinance that the chief of the district police would be paid a monthly wage of 1000 Pengö; the sub-chief of police 800 Pengö; the chief of the district office 700 Pengö; the police inspectors 600 Pengö; the public guardians, the secretaries, the cashiers, the translators etc. 400 Pengö[48]. In the district of Cluj, the documents make mention of the fact that some guardians got monthly wages that could be up to 600 Pengö[49].

Immediately after their setting up, these legions have been confronted with a large number of problems. Thus, beginning with the 26th of December 1944, on the basis of a proceedings signed by the Allied Control Commission, it has started the reducing of the gendarmes unit's effectives from northern Transylvania. This protocol has given rise to virulent protests on the part of many sub-units, the officers of which expressed their fear of future purifications and the dissatisfacion for the fact that their pecuniary rights for the last months have not been payed off. The soldiers were also dissatisfied of the fact that they were concentrated for a long time, away from their families, which were faced, most of them, with serious difficulties[50].

The future of the Romanian gendarmerie from northern Transylvania has not improved significantly, either, after the installation of the government led by Petru Groza, the Soviets obstructing the immediate return in the territory of the Romanian public order troops. In its turn, the Groza government, also, has shown no interest to support the demands of the public order structures that requested to reinstate themselves immediately in northern Transylvania, because their return might have inconvenienced the programme of introducing their own confidential people within these institutions[51]. In fact,there was only from the 10th of July 1945 that the gendarmes formations which had been forced to leave their units in the autumn of 1944 have returned in the territory[52].

The forced evacuation of the northern Transylvania's authorities has created difficulties not only with regard to the ensuring of the internal order, but also with respect to the frontier's guarding. Thus, due to the missing of the frontier guards and of the custom-house officials, the line of the frontier established at Trianon proved to be, actually, non-existent, allowing the entrance in northern Transylvania and, from there, into Romania, of a great number of forcign currency, which was prejudicing the national currency, by its exchange[53]. Also, by the abolition of the frontier imposed by the Vienna Award, foreign citizens that could not be subjected to a rigorous customs checking were frequently entering within the Romanian territory [54].

*

As for the attitude of ***the ethnic minorities*** from the territory towards the recent state of affairs, the withdrawal of northern Transylvania out of the Bucharest government's administration in the autumn of 1944 has been greeted, to a certain extent, by the Hungarians and the Jews and regarded with anxiety and fear by the Germans.

The Hungarians have divided in two categories with regard to the attitude towards the new state of affairs in northern Transylvania. Part of them have lost their hope in the winning of the war by the Germans as the battle-front moved off and have begun to adhere to leftist political organizations. On the 6th of October 1944, The Hungarian People's Union (U.P.M.) has been formed in Braşov, an organization to the creation of which an important part have been played by the south-eastern Transylvanian structures of the M.A.D.O.S.Z. (also known as the Group of Braşov). The new organization, led by Kurko Gyarfas, has associated, for legitimacy, members of the former Hungarian Party of the inter-war period. Any democrat or national-democrat Hungarian of over 18 could become member of that organization. Because the organization was to have its centers in the districts capitals, it was required that the majority of the members would reside in the capitals of the districts[55]. The same day, the U.P.M. has adhered to the National Democrat Front (F.N.D.), the newspaper ***Scânteia*** publishing, on the 8th of October 1944, the adhesion of this formation to the F.N.D.'s programme. That fact has provoked the immediate reaction of the National Peasant Party, which has published on the 11th of October in its newspaper ***Dreptatea*** on the front page an article headed «The Madosz wants to enter the government, too». The article, signed by Corneliu Coposu, has brought many accusations to the Hungarian leaders, for their attitude.

In northern Transylvania, these organizations have found pretty soon sympathizers.

Thus, on the 22nd of October 1944, local organizations of the M.A.D.O.S.Z. have been set up, that have evolved and have had a position more or less independent to the center. In Cluj, Sunday the 22nd of October, during the forming meeting of M.A.D.O.S.Z., presided by Kos Karoly, Szepessy Sandor and Haphazi Samu, it has been decided «the creation of a people's academy, for the diffusion and the explanation of the democratic tenets within the vast masses of the people»[56].

As for the U.P.M., organization that was supported by most of the leftist Hungarians and that had the advantage of an excellent collaboration with the Communist Party, its activity has extended in northern Transylvania beginning with the 23rd of November 1944[57]. Also, there were formed local structures of the Romanian Social Democrat Party (P.S.D.R.) and of the Communist Party. In fact, beginning with the end of October and in November, there has been taking place the passing from the Hungarian Communist Party's structures to the local communist structures of the Transylvanian Hungarians. They would merge eventually with the Romanian Communist Party, fact that has given rise to disagreements and contradictions inside the Hungarian community. The most ardent adversary of this fusion was Jordaki Lajos. Initially, the local organizations of the M.A.D.O.S.Z. have refused to transform themselves into the U.P.M. and even after they have been overwhelmed by the center of Braşov, under pressure, they have still tried to keep their authonomy. The reality was that the small local organizations have had the sympathy of the inhabitants because they knew better the local problems and were more bound and, at the same time, they had a certain independence and liberty of action from the center.

The statute of Transylvania has been a question of priority for the leadership of the U.P.M. and the showing of the Soviet model has benefited, as for the settlement of the ethnic problems, by a privileged place in the U.P.M. representatives' speeches, especially in the ones that were published in the official press of the Union[58]. In the leftist Hungarian newspapers there have appeared statements of the following type: «In the Soviet Union there are no majority or minority nations», «All the peoples may live freely their national identity, their own cultural life», «All the peoples may live freely their immovable fraternal identity even during the greatest dangers. None of them has thought of secession, of teasing the great union of the socialist community». These slogans, published many times next to the complete or partial presentation of the Soviet constitution, was pursuing to gain the people's trust for the leftist parties and organizations[59]. The National Democrat Front, and generally the Romanian political left, appeared to be the protector of the nationalities. Within the Union, it has begun to show the interest for popularizing the Soviet government's speeches and those of the Romanian leftist parties[60]. In this way, the taking of the power by the Romanian political leftism has become, in the opinion of the U.P.M.'s leadership, the key to settle the Transylvanian question. Thus, the Armisticeb Convention and especially its 19th article, by which it was stipulated the return of northern Transylvania to the Romanian state, provided the installation of a «democratic» government (a leftist one), was considered to be a just and adequate act. Banyai Laszlo showed that only an integration in a democratic Romania would guarantee the equality of rights of the nationalities and would put an end to the chauvinism. He also affirmed that the political Left, once it got the power, «would replace the ethnic crumbling by the great unity»[61]. Thus, the leadership of the U.P.M has insisted on the coalition of the Hungarian community with the Romanian political leftism in reproving the projects of an autonomous Transylvania. There were frequently coming out in the press articles that seconded this idea. For example, in «Vilogossag» of the 10th of December 1944, it has been published an article signed by Nagy Istvan that reproved the ones who militated in favour of the autonomy of Transylvania. He was trying to rally the Hungarian community to the struggle led by the socialist movement, with the slogan « No to the Northern-Transylvanian Republic, yes to democracy»[62].

The U.P.M. leaders presented the F.N.D. as being the only one able to respect the Armistice Convention and its governing as the only one that would provide the equality of rights for all citizens; thus, Transylvania could become a motherland of the Hungarians and, at the same time, part of a democratic Romania. This judgment has been decisive in the shaping of the U.P.M.'s official standpoint, for which the coming to power of the F.N.D. meant the guarantee of the success of this organization's efforts to represent the Hungarian interest in Romania.

The U.P.M. has delegated a commission to study the nationalities law's project proposed by the F.N.D. and has organized a conference for debating the question of the Cluj Hungarian University and has intensified its approachs to the Romanian political Left in order to settle the problems of the southern Transylvanian Hungarians. As for the possibility of setting up the autonomy and the partial revision of the borders, the leadership of the U.P.M. has suggested the juridical integration of the Transylvanian Hungarian community within the «democratic» Romania[63].

Because most of the U.P.M.'s leaders were from southern Transylvania and even from the Old Kingdom's territory, they considered that any modification of the borders that would offer parts of Transylvania to Hungary would also weaken the Hungarian community from Romania and would render difficult the collaboration with the majority population. Thus, the best strategy, from the U.P.M.'s point of view, was an alliance with the F.N.D. in order to obtain the administrative autonomy, the right to use the Hungarian language, Hungarian reviewers by the ministries, an united and numerous Hungarian community, with solid economic foundations[64].

At the opposite pole to the U.P.M., there was that part of the Hungarian population that spoke on every occasion of the imminence of the borders modification in the favour of Hungary and that showed an open hostility towards the Bucharest authorities[65]. During the last months of 1944 and in 1945, there were heard rumours about the cease of a few cities and regions from Transylvania to Hungary (like the cities of Carei, Satu-Mare, Sighetul Marmației and Oradea)[66].

There were some rumours among the Hungarians about the organization of a plebiscite for the creation of a Transylvanian republic[67]. There was also talking of the existence of an agreement (especially on the eve of the Hungarian – Russian armistice negotiations) according to which Hungary and Transylvania, entirely, were to become independent republics, under the sovereignty of the Soviet Union, with a statute somehow similar to the one that was planned for the Baltic states. At the same time, within the Hungarian political circles from Transylvania, it was beginning to talk more and more often, after the signing of the Russian – Hungarian armistice, about the discontentment of the Soviet Military Command by the Bucharest authorities, that they blame for not being able to ensure the country's order. There would have been intervened an agreement between the Soviets and the Debrecen government in this way, they said, by which it was planned to send Hungarian police and gendarmerie forces to keep the order in northern Transylvania. Within the university environment – that interpreted the projects regarding the creation of a Danubian Federation according to its own wishes – it was spreading the idea that a Great Hungary would soon be created, «larger than ever before, governed by a people's democratic government, established in Moscow, and by local provincial governments holding limited competence». There were also rumours according to which the leaders of the Hungarian community would be requested by the Soviets to help at the overthrowing of all non-democratic formations from Transylvania.

That kind of rumours gave rise to a powerful echo in the Romanian public opinion, the pessimism and the depression becoming more and more pronounced, fact that could represent the premise of some desperate actions. That was the more so as, after the short period of time when the Romanian authorities have been established in a few northern Transylvanian districts, many Hungarian civil servants that had held positions during the Horthist regime, too, were reinstated in their jobs. Also, the inscriptions in Hungarian were kept on, the official documents were drawn up in the same language and were having as headings the word «Magyarorszag» and King Stephen's Crown, the stamps were in Hungarian, also etc.

In villages there were appearing leaflets by which the Hungarian youth was requested not to present for conscription in the Romanian Army. In a report of the 13th of November 1944, forwarded to the Chairmanship of the Council of Ministers by the War Minister, it was drawn the attention upon the fact that the young men of Hungarian nationality from the district of Mureş refused to present themselves for recruitment. The respective young men have been recruited in absence (according to the 69th article of the recruitment law), being sanctioned to satisfy a three years military service[68]. Similar situations also occurred in the districts of Trei Scaune, Ciuc, Maramureş and Odorhei. The recruiting council has convicted the perpetrators according to the 43rd article of the recruitment law, that also punished the ones who enabled to youngmen to elude the provisions of the law with a penalty of three to ten years imprisonment and a fine of 10000 to 100000 lei[69]. Part of the merchants and of the Hungarian staff employed in the public institutions were giving proof of provocative attitudes, using the Hungarian language, inclusively in the correspondence with the Romanian churches[70].

As for the relations between the Hungarian population and the Red Army soldiers, it was noticed that they were relatively good, in many cases, the Hungarians passing by in silence, by spirit of discipline, the drawbacks of the occupation regime, thing that could not to be said of the Romanians. In fact, at the same time with their re-appointment in the administrative and economic life of northern Transylvania, the leaders of the Hungarian population from this territory have tried, by all possible means, to gain the full confidence of the Soviet military authorities[71]. In the district of Mureş, the relations between the Hungarians and the Soviets were definetely better than the ones between the Romanians and the Soviets, the contrast being easy to notice by observers. The city of Reghin has been the only one where the Romanian element has succeeded in gaining the sympathy of the Soviet Command. As for the rest of the district, inclusively in Târgu-Mureş, the things have happened in a completely different way, the consistent insistences of the Hungarians coming off victorious[72]. Also, reports of the Gendarmes Inspectorates in the territory recorded that the Soviet soldiers were spending more time in the entourage of the Hungarian inhabitants, while towards the Romanians they had a hostile attitude[73].

Actually, right after the 23rd of August 1944, the Hungarian Crown Council and government had planned a strategy of national diversion in Transylvania, which was pursuing, as an immediate and of long standing effect, the keeping of the Transylvanian territory occupied on the 30th of August 1940. The government from Budapest and the provisional government of Debrecen have both suggested the Transylvanian Hungarians to create a communist party so that, in case of the advance of the Red Army in the province, the Soviet authorities would find a center of political and doctrinary fidelity in the Hungarians minority and would entrust it the governing of northern Transylvania[74]. It has come thus to the situation where the adhering to the communist party would be done, in northern Transylvania, especially under the impulse of ethnic nature interests. According to an informative note of the 25th of January 1945 (that represents a synthesis of what has been recorded in northern Transylvania during December 1944 and January 1945) of the Braşov Gendarmes Legion's Commander, sent to the Prime Minister Nicolae Rădescu, there were emphasized the following facts:

1) – The Hungarians, assembled in M.A.D.O.S.Z., insisted around the Soviet authorities on the creation of an atmosphere of sympathy, in order to get the autonomy of the entire Transylvania. And that was due to the fact that there was some idea among the Hungarians that «the entire Transylvania would better be under any domination, provided that the Romanian one would be gone»[75];

2) – they have done their best for this action, taking care that any caprice of the Soviet commanders would be satisfied, regardless of the sacrifices and their political allegiance;

3) – at the same time, the recruiting of the Hungarian youngmen has begun, for the strengthening of the civil guards in every locality, part of the units thus formed were even sent to the battle-front;

4) – there was some talking about the fact that there would be resumed the discussions regarding the statute of Transylvania, after the communist government of Debrecen will establish in Budapest;

5) – it was initiated the organization of gendarmes troops, formed of young Hungarians and border guards, that would constitute, alongside the communist civil guards, the elements to ensure the guard of the northern Transylvanian territory. Equipped with good armament, those troops were to be used, if needed, inclusively against the Romanian Army. This «police army» that was to operate at the borders and in the interior of the territory was paid through the contribution of the inhabitants. Their regimentals was marked by the presence of the Soviet communist badge, instead of the military badge.[76]

It was also found that, by taking advantage of their special relationships with Soviets, the Hungarians that have been in the the Soviet Union and spoke Russian have committed robberies in various places, especially in the area of Cluj. They were putting on Soviet military clothes and were stealing from the remote villages and hamlets and, in case of eventual encounters with the representatives of the civil guards in the territory, the same Soviet regimentals offered them an excellent protection[77].

It was not the whole Hungarian population in northern Transylvania that rally to the actions supported by a part of their leaders. In many reports and informative notes of the authorities, there can be find mentions concerning the existence of some cases in which the Soviets have shown no indulgence to the Hungarians. For example, in January 1945, 14 Hungarians were arrested and confined in the camp of Sâmpetru (district of Braşov), for they have openly demonstrated against the Red Army and the Soviet Union. Germans were also confined in that camp and they were deported later on in the Soviet Union. The Hungarians were not deported but they have stayed in the camp for approximately one year. A report from July 1945 noticed that only the sick ones were released.

At the same time, police reports made mention of an accentuation of the anti-Hungarian feelings harboured by the Romanians, feelings that manifested especially on the occasion of national and historical commemoration days (for instance, the 1st of December or the 24th of January)[78], but also on the occasion of the return of many Romanians from refuge, when they found that both their former jobs and their homes were occupied, mostly, by Hungarians[79].

The Jews that succeeded to escape, one way or another, from the fate of their conationals deported in the nazi concentration camps have gathered together into local and regional Jewish communities and, on the 21st of October 1944, they have sent their representatives to Cluj, where they have put the basis of the «National Jewish Community», assembled in the building of the Jewish public hospital. During the meeting, thc speakers have expressed their feelings of gratitude towards the liberating Soviet and Romanian Armies, emphasizing the fact that «they are ready to cooperate with the Romanian population and with the Hungarian minority, without resentments and vengeance, for the construction of Transylvania»[80]. They have even regarded with sympathy the arrival of the Red Army, being, aside the Hungarians, among the first to adhere to the communist party's structures. Dr. Moses Rosen noticed that the Romanian Jews have felt a great gratitude towards the Soviet Union and he has shared the same feeling. That was not because they have accepted the Soviet ideology, but because they understood that the Soviets were the ones to save their lifes. He also noticed that many Jews have become ardent communists, either by conviction, or by opportunism. Part of them have arrived at the leadership of the party and even in the government[81].

Simultaneously with the actions of the Jews from northern Transylvania, the Chief Rabbi of the Jewish community from Romania addressed to Vishinsky in Bucharest, on the occasion of his call in Romania in November 1944. He has asked for his support in liberating the Jews native of northern Transylvania, deported and confined in work camps in Hungary during the Horthist regime and that have been captured yet by the Soviet forces during the military developments inside the Hungarian territory[82]. During November and December 1944, the main efforts of the Jewish community leaders Dr. A. Safran and Dr. W. Filderman have concentrated on the repatriation of the surviving Jews native of northern Transylvania[83]. In Cluj, at the very end of October 1944, 50 persons from the Hungarian labour detachments have returned home. But those who could return home by the end of 1944 were very few. An optician from the city, supported by the authorities, has succeeded in setting out a train, with its own locomotive, that was used to repatriate the Jews[84]. According to the statistic data of the Jewish World Congress, there were 16.763 Jews in Cluj in 1942. In 1944, at the beginning of the deportations, according to unofficial statistics, there were 18.000 Jews. In July 1945, their number was of only 1000. There were no married couples among those who have returned. Children, very few[85].

The adhering of the Jews to the communist party, in addition to some abuses committed by them with the aid of the Soviet soldiers, have provoked hostile feelings among the local population. The fact that the lamp oil, very necessary during the winter, had become a serious problem, especially in the countryside, is well-known. It seems that the Jews from the villages have represented an important part of the oil speculators, oil that was often obtained from the Soviet soldiers, reselling it at very high prices (500-1000 lei per litre), inaccessable for an important part of the population. The peasants, shocked at this trade, wondered «how come that the honest merchants cannot get a drop of oil, while the Jews have large amounts of that liquid, that they speculate in an inhuman manner»[86]. The mayors of the villages had addressed many complaints to the district authorities, to the Soviet authorities in the area and even to the High Commissary, drawing the attention upon the hostility manifested by the population towards those Jews who passed all bounds in their zeal to gain money. It was also made mention of the fact that many of the Jews were alive due to exactly the same inhabitants that they now exploit. A peasant from the village of Jucu (district of Cluj) declared that in his village and the surroundings «some Jews gentlemens and dandies are walking by, followed by Russian soldiers, telling us that we are all the same if we adhere to the democrats and, because this call did not work, they have sent us to the notary's offices and served out wheat at a price of 28 Pengö (840 lei) per bushel, but only for those who adhere, while those who do not enroll for the democrat's lists get nothing or in case that they give wheat to any of them, they give it for the price of 56 Pengö, that is exactly double. Because there are still very few Romanians that enter their names, these agents threaten that the ones who do not enter their names will be deported in Siberia»[87]. The sayings of the peasant were checked up and confirmed by many other peasants from another four neighbouring villages[88].

At the same time, both in the cities and in the villages, it was found that the Jews that became members of the communist party carry Russian revolvers and some of them even automatic pistols and «they are not doing it discreetly, on the contrary, they have found the opportunity to act in such a manner that the coat, which covers the gun at the belt, would move aside, as if involuntarily, so that the eyes of the people around them would see the gun. These Jews, armed with guns, travel all over the villages and make people adhere to the communist party in return for one or two litres of lamp oil, that they sell at 50-60 lei and the people from the country does enroll. These things are happening by daylight in the entire district of Cluj»[89].

Abuses of that kind have led to the growing of the anti-Semitism, both in the cities and in villages. There were people that considered, at the beginning of 1945, that the Jews have returned to their native localities only in order to revenge on the Hungarians, for the things they had to undergo during the Horthyst regime[90]. Then, perhaps as a consequence of the behaviour of some Jews, on the 7th of March 1945, when the survivors of the concentration camps have returned in

Cluj, among the city's inhabitants there have occured some manifestations of hostility. Thus, «the evening of March the 6th 1945, it was announced through the trade unions that on the 7th of March will arrive the first group of Jews of the 15000 Jews from Galicia, Poland and Prussia and from other regions under German influence, where they had been deported from Cluj and Hungary. The union's leadership has asked its members to send somebody from their families to the railway station on the 7th of March, with food, in order to give a warm welcome to those that are returning home. I addressed to a group of women (we're talking about a journalist from Cluj, whose name is not mentioned, nor his nationality or his age, author's annotation) that seemed to be worker's wives and I asked what is all this big meeting about and why do they bustle. That's why, one of them replies, they carry us along as if we are some kind of lunatics, those people from the trade union our husbands are enrolled in, that is we are compelled to welcome our brothers of Mosaic religion who have been deported by the Germans an year ago... But when they have taken them away, another one from the group said, they made us spit on them and swear them like a trooper. But how come they return, I asked, when everybody said that the Germans have killed them all, have sent them in the other world. They did, another one answered, that's what they say, but you see, sir, excuse me, comrade or however I am supposed to call you, there are dead people that resurrect before the judgment day»[91]. Because the train that was to bring the Jews was delayed a few hours, the crowd gathered in the railway station had begun to leave. The journalist noticed yet another fact from which we can perceive the anti-Semitism and the inter-ethnic tensions existing in Transylvania in that period: «...a woman ask another one if she will return to the railway station later on. The latter replied, yelling – What do you think? Am I to let my household's things for some bonelazy Jews that drove us to poverty? Let the union eat them unroasted, we for ourselves, we need peace, bread, boots and things to cover our impoverished homes...»[92]

Generally speaking, of all the inhabitants of northern Transylvania, the Jews have had the best relations with the Soviets (except for the robberies done by the ordinary soldiers, that made no allowance for anybody and for nothing) and the leaders of this community have got a real support. Thus, as early as in November 1944, it was created, about the Commissariate for the administration of the liberated regions of Transylvania, a special service for the Jewish problems from the liberated Transylvanian territories, the prerogatives of which were to be the following: 1) – to organize the work of assisting the Jews left in the liberated Transylvanian territory or returned there and being poverty-stricken; 2) – to collect data regarding the properties from northern Transylvania, that had belonged to Romanian citizens of Jewish ethnic origin, abusively dispossessed by the Hungarian racist legislation. This service was to make proposals in this way, concerning the inventory and the conservation of these properties and, also, the manner of their retrocession to the legal owners; 3) – to make proposals regarding the remedy of the anti-Jewish law's effects of the Horthyst period; 4) – to collect data regarding the Jews deported by the Hungarian authorities and to look for the appropriate means to bring back in the country the survivors. It has been decided that this service, according to the decision of the High Commissary, would be led by a technical consultant and the expenses would be covered by the commissariate's budget. After a short time, Dr. Ernest Marton, former deputy, was charged with the leading of the service[93].

In the beginning of 1945, the Jewish Democratic Committee has been created in Cluj, which, although has functioned in the shadow of the communist party, has strived for the returned Jews to be able to re-enter their homes and to get back the properties that have been taken from them. However, it has been found that many Jewish properties were requisitioned by the Hungarian financial administration and transported to Hungary during 1944[94].

The Jewish Democratic Committee has taken care to provide living conditions for the Jews returned from the concentration camps. They were accommodated in Peter Hall villa, next to Canalul Morii. A canteen and a hospital (nowadays Medicala III) were opened. The Jewish education institutions have been re-opened only in 1946, the few existing children being enrolled to Romanian or Hungarian schools[95]. From 1945 to 1953, the Committee has published in Cluj a review, first named «Unitatea» and then «Drum nou». The review was reflecting the Jewish life, but it was clearly having an anti-Zionist and anti-emigrationist orientation. It was led by the P.C.R. (the Romanian Communist Party)[96].

At the same time, in every district, at the level of every city or village, there have been appointed persons that were commissioned to gather and inventory the Jewish assets, to transport and deposit them.

A large part of those assets has been restored to the surviving owners, but, on the other hand, most of the goods have passed in the patrimony of some institutions, of some persons or have simply been taken by the Soviet soldiers and transported beyond the Russian borders[97].

As for **the Germans**, they were the ones that have suffered the most on account of the presence of the Red Army's troops. Immediately after the liberation of northern Transylvania, according to the requests of the Allied Control Commission, addressed both to the Chairmanship of the Council of Ministers and to the local authorities of every district, the Germans were mobilized to forced labour. The mobilization was done by the police structures in the cities and by the gendarmes organs in the countryside. The organization of battalions or labour settlements has been left at the charge of the General Command of the Territory, through the Territorial Circles. For this purpose, it has been decided that the police and the gendarmerie would forward to the respective Territorial Circles nominal lists that would comprise all those to be mobilized – men and women. The age of 17 to 45 has been established as a mobilization criterion for men and 18 to 30 for women[98].

With the view of organizing men labour battalions, the General Command of the Territory within the framework of the General Headquarters has given dispositions to the Territorial Corps by means of which it has been specified that the mobilized men would be integrated in labour and utilities formations by the existing detachments from the country, in order to perform work for the railways, roads, bridges etc. These detachments have functioned under the direct control of the General Headquarters[99]. The General Command of the Territory has ordered the Territorial Corps that the units formed of women will be rendered to the Territorial Corps by the police and gendarmes organs and will be placed at the disposal of the State authorities which would decide about their utilisation in various activities – through the prefect's offices. The units with effectives of 50 to 100 women will be used for the works of railway and roads maintenance, in hospitals and in factories, for the work in the fields etc.[100]

The mobilization was made in five hours from the moment the orders were conveyed. All the people to be mobilized had to prepare their luggages with the needed clothes: summer and winter clothes, footwear, clean linen, bed clothes and dishes, also the food needed for a twenty days period. The whole luggage was not to exceed 150 kilogrammes for person. The transportation was to be made by trucks, according to the ordinances, but in fact the cases in which trucks were place at the disposal of the German population were very few. The mothers with babies at the breast were exempted from the work. The minor children of the mobilized ones were to be attended by the relatives or, in their absence, were under the care of the cityhalls or of the prefect's offices. All those to be mobilized were compelled to have upon them identity papers. Their properties were left under the custody of the cityhalls[101]. They were left to be administered by the cityhalls until October 1945, when the Patriotic Defense Central Committee of Bucharest required that the goods left from the Transylvanian Germans that have abandoned their domiciles or that have been confined and deported are to be rendered to the respective organization[102].

A special category of Germans, that have been subjected later to extremely strict conditions, were the ones called «the dangerous». They were confined, initially, in the camp of Târgu-Jiu, then they were sent to the Soviet Union. Among the so-called «dangerous people» were:

a) – the leader of the German ethnic group, Andreas Schmid, together with his main assistants and the most important members of all the organizations at his orders, also all the leaders of the German minority that have distinguished themselves and have shown anti-Romanian opinions;

b) – The leaders of the German youth paramilitary formations and of the Hitler Jugend. The members of these groups have been disarmed and their guns were rendered to the closest garrisons;

c) – The youngmen of German ethnic origin, Romanian citizens that had been enlisted in S.S. or Wehrmacht units. (The police reports took notice of the fact that these youngmen have returned in the country with the guns they have received at the time of the recruiting, guns that were hidden in various places);

d) – The military elements that were thought to be dangerous, even if they had not been official leaders of various organizations[103].

Generally speaking, the majority of the German population has been subjected to a strict detention or surveillance regime. Those that have remained «free» in the localities, very few and mostly women, children and old people, have integrated themselves with the new order and have not tried to undermine the authorities[104].

Beginning with January 1945, it was recorded the deportation of the German population to the work camps in the Soviet Union. The Swabians from the North-West of the country have represented a significant part of the deported population of German ethnic origin. On the 6th of January 1945, in the note no. 031 emitted by the Allied Control Commission, it has been ordered the deportation of the Romanian citizens of German origin to the work camps of the Soviet Union, men aged from 17 to 45 and women from 18 to 30[105]. In 1945, there have been deported over 4000 Swabians from the area of Satu-Mare and almost 1000 of them have died[106]. Assimilated by the communist ideology with the fascists, their deportation has coincided with the actions of pursuing and arresting the fascist of the district of Satu-Mare. The consequences of the deportations have reflected directly upon the demographic situation of the region. In a document drawn up by the prefect's office of the district of Satu-Mare, concerning the demographic situation during February and March 1945, it has been found that the number of the Swabian population has significantly decreased[107]. In the actions of deportation, there were not included only persons of German ethnic origin, however, but also Romanians[108], because, it was wanted, at the Soviets requests, mainly the achievement of the needed number of concentrated people. The number of the deported people had to be fulfiled and, on several occasions, it was completed with persons of a different ethnic origin.

*

By bringing up a few aspects of ethnic nature from northern Transylvania during the period of the administration submitted to the Soviet control, we cannot go on without making mention of the state of mind of the region's population regarding **the shifting and the quartering of the Soviet troops throughout the localities**.

The questions concerning the relations between the Soviet forces, the civil population and the Romanian state, after the 23rd of August 1944, concerning their behaviour represent a chapter that only during the last few years could attract the attention of the historians and of the public. During the communist regime, it has been tried to give credit to the image of a liberating Red Army which deserved all the eulogies, while the inconvenient evidences regarding the presence of the Soviet troops in Romania were being passed by in silence. Only after 1989, when a large part of the archive documents have been accessible to the researchers, it has been noticed that the reports of the gendarmerie, of the police, the prefect's offices, the cityhalls etc. were abounding in notes concerning the abuses committed by the Soviet Army. That army, though being in the Romanian territory as an allied army, did not always act as such. There have been registered denunciations everywhere the Soviets had arrived, both from the civil population and the local authorities[109].

In the situation created after the removal of northern Transylvania from the Romanian administration, the governments from Bucharest and the Romanian political leaders have tried to prevent, in general, any conflict with the Soviets, demanding the population not to respond to the provocations and, especially, to avoid the outbreak of some bloody incidents[110]. Thus, by a series of circular orders of the autumn of 1944, it has been required to the civilians and to the military that everyone would contribute, during that exceedingly severe conditions the country was passing through, to «the consolidation of the comradeship with the Soviet allies»[111], would accomplish the legal dispositions required by the Russians, would support the requisitions, the supplying, the quartering of the troops and, if possible, would satisfy on the spot any legal demand of the Soviet soldiers[112].

From the existing documents, from the spoken or written testimonies of the contemporaries, the worry and the anxiety of the population towards the passing and the quartering of the Russian troops throughout the localities could be easily noticed. It has been made mention of the population's fear of walking in the streets after sunset or of going to work in the fields, especially with horses and waggons, because the Soviet soldiers were sequestering by force both animals and persons, that they force to transport them dozens of kilometers away. The inhabitants were not feeling safe even in their own houses, because lonely soldiers were entering by force in their homes, many times, disturbing the family's peace and stealing the owner's properties[113]. Also, many documents record the thefts committed by the Russians, the reports containing endless lists with the names of the injured inhabitants, their domiciles and the total value of the goods taken by force. Among the latters, we mention only some of them, in order to offer an image of their diversity – waggons, domestic goods, clothes, body linen, eiderdowns, towels, automobiles, money, animals, cereals, fowls etc.

This kind of illegal requisitions and abuses have taken place in every district of northern Transylvania, in every locality the Soviets had passed through or had been stationed. In this way, we evoke for exemplification part of the account of Gustav Zikeli (member of the delegation of the Bistriţa's Saxons that have taken part to the national convention of the 1st of December 1918 from Alba Iulia, former employee in various positions of that cityhall from 1936) regarding the presence of the Soviet soldiers in the city of Bistriţa: «...There were not ordered formations that came, but soldiers – isolated Russians, at a distance of approximately twenty steps from one to another, each of them holding their guns ready to fire. Every fourth or fifth was a woman, also in military uniform and with the gun ready to fire... The soldiers have arrived to the national bank, where they have waited for the rest of the troops. When these troops have arrived, they have spread in the neighbouring houses and, later on, in the whole city...the Russians have come to us and asked for alcoholic liquors, as everywhere... The Russian troops have probably had a 24 hours break in Bistriţa, because in the morning of the 14th of October, at seven o'clock, most of the soldiers, not the oficers, have started to move on. Our uninvited guests have left, too, only after they have opened the door from our room. I have seen them taking from the house two or three armchairs, probably in order to seat more comfortably. As for the rest, everything was alright inside the house. It was not until I get to the front court that I have seen the damages... Everything has been checked up from top to bottom... Our valuables, the gold, the silver, a dinner set of silver, two hundred gold nibs for fountain pens and other things, the money as well, have dissapeared. They have left us only the things that could get broken...The afternoon of the 14th of October, two Headquarters officers, a colonel and a major have come together with their wives and their two children in our house. The officers have asked for food and wine. We still had one or two litres of wine but no food. The guests have stuck off a hen for supper, that was cooked by the orderly. We have all sit to table, including the orderly, and the colonel has shared the meal... During that night there were some gunshots in the neighbouring house, for an oil lamp. There was no electricity, so that an oil lamp was a very wanted object. The next morning, the colonel has explained to us that we had to leave the house. The civilians were not allowed to live in a house occupied by Headquarters officers... When we left, the colonel has assured us that he would leave everything intact... When we returned to our home, there were three subalterns instead of the two Headquarters officers. After the departure of the Headquarters officers, they have established in our house arbitrarily. When we have showed up, they have left to their former house. We did not know, of course, whether the subalterns have come in immediately after the Headquarters officers have left or if the house has remained uninhabited, too, for a while. We have realized that all the clothes and the food were missing. All the furniture has remained...»[114] Anyway, the houses were not the only places to be robbed, as the Soviets have taken away everything they could from schools and churches, too. In a vilage from the district of Bihor, for instance, there have been stolen goods of a total value that exceeded 900.000 lei[115], while the number of injured inhabitants was of over 150, the total value of the confiscated goods exceeding the amount of 12.000.000 lei[116].

There were reported serious troubles with regard to the requisition of the animals, because they represented for many families the only source of food and means of labour. According to the 11th article of the Armistice Convention, the Romanian state was obliged to deliver animals to the Russians. There have been commandeered cattle, sheep, horses and fowls. In general, the number of the animals requested by the Soviets was very large, many of the localities being unable to satisfy their claims. From the territory of the region Hilda alone (district of Cluj) there have been requisioned the following: horses – 76, to a value of 26.580.000 lei; cattle – 26, to a value of 9.604.000 lei; sheep – 1257, to a value of 22.651.000 lei; pigs – 1208, to a value of 30.274.000 lei; fowls – 188, to a value of 72.000 lei, and also many other things, such as: domestic utilities, automobiles, beverages, food, fodder, furniture, clothes etc. – the total amount of the goods taken from this administrative unit running to 102.327.683 lei[117]. From the city of Cluj and the surroundings, the Soviets have requisitioned in the autumn of 1944 19 horses, 10 cows, 3 calves, 8 pigs and 102 sheep, all these animals amounting to 29.190.000 lei[118]. From the region of Aleşd, in the period from 21st of September 1944 until the 15th of June 1945, there have been taken over 320 horses, 134 cattle, 369 pigs and 447 sheep and from the region Oradea, district of Bihor, in the same period, there have been requisitioned 9090 horses, 1108 cattle, 1296 sheep and 3570 pigs. Generally speaking, under the protection of the laws that favoured them, the Russians have committed many abuses, especially in requisioning horses and cattle – the horses being very needed both in transportation and in the military operations developments. In the district of Bihor alone, the number of horses taken by the Soviet Army has amounted to almost half of the sum stipulated for the entire country[119], while from the district of Năsăud, until the 9th of November 1944, there have already been requisitioned 898 waggons altogether with their horses[120].

All those requisitions of goods, money, animals and food – part of them imposed by the stipulations of the Armistice Convention and part of them illegal – have been born very hard by the inhabitants. There have been noticed cases when many families have preferred to kill their animals instead of being taken by the Russians[121], action that have often represented the cause for scuffles between soldiers and civilians. Also, it should not be forget the fact that the inhabitants of northern Transylvania had had to bear, for four years, numerous deprivations on the part of the Horthyst regime, so that the Russian's requisitions have brought the local inhabitants in a state of mind close to despair. For instance, we reproduce the request of the people from the village of Văleni, district of Cluj, from which we mention the following: «The people of our village hss almost run short of animals, as it has been taken away in 1943 a number of 102 animals and in the autumn of 1944 12 cattle, 70 sheep and 6 pigs. All these years, there have been taken from us almost all the cereals. For the carrying out of the truce between Russia and Romania, we have given until now 12 cattle, 78 sheep and 7 pigs. The village has a population of 784 souls, being thus pretty small. Considering the geographic location of our village, at an altitude from 750 to 879 metres, the soil of which does not produce corn, nor enough wheat, but only bad spring oat and potatoes and that depends on the weather, and the fact that part of the village inhabitants live from the breeding of animals and from the labour of the forest. The forests are almost gone and, when the animals will be taken proportionately with the neighbouring villages which did not endure as much as we have, then our inhabitants are to leave their homes and go in other parts of the country in order to earn their living, because they have but 2 or 3 animals for yoke, reproduction and for milk, two owners grouping together for an yoke, helping each other for the tilling of the ground. In order to stop this precarious condition of our people, we ask you to intervene so that, in the future, we should have smaller quotas for animals that are to be rendered to the procurement center...»[122] This request, addressed to the prefect's office, has been signed by the mayor of that village, Băros Tudor, by the sub-mayor and by other persons.

The abuses committed by the Soviets were numerous, fact that made the Allied Control Commission take action, beginning with December 1944, for the limitation of the injustices committed to the population. Thus, the Allied Control Commission, through the General Inspectorates of the Gendarmerie, has ordered that the Soviet troops would give receipts to the people whose various goods were requisitioned. The order was signed by the chief of the Economic Department of the Allied Control Commission and by the chief of the Supplies Group, Lieutenant Colonel Vervkin. By the address no. 1104/ 1944, there were stipulated the legal conditions of procuring some goods by the Soviet Army, the introduction of a model document, that would be given by the Soviet military units when they receive the goods, being now necessary. The Soviets had to give receipts to the one that rendered the goods, with the heading and the stamp of the military unit's field post and the signature of the unit's commander[123]. In addition to that, it has been decided the issue of a giving – receiving receipt, in three copies, one of them being received by the the one that rendered the goods, the second by the one that requisitioned and the third had to be attached to the invoice that were forwarded to the ministry. They had to have the legible signatures of both the giver and the receiver. If the receiver had no seal, then the receipts were authenticated by the seal of the Soviet military command of that region or by that of the Allied Control Commission's mandatory in that district. These documents were to be translated from Romanian into Russian and from Russian into Romanian, by the existing translator of the Soviet military units. However, it was specified that the lack of a translator was no obstacle for handing over the receipts[124].

Despite all these, the abuses committed by the Russian soldiers not only did not stop, but on the contrary, they continued and even increased, fact that results from the new orders given in the beginning of 1945. Thus, by an order from February the 14th 1945, it was mentioned that there had to be drawn up reports that would comprise the following: a) – the name and the address of the person that was subjected to the notified requisition of goods or to the abuse; b) – the date and the location where that fact has happened; c) – the manner those goods have been taken (in exchange for a receipt, for money, without any formality, on the grounds that those goods were of Soviet origin or that they were German war material, and also thc circumstances that abuse has been committed); d) – clues about the Soviet soldiers to whom that fact was attributed, the number of the military field post, of the unit, the rank, the name and the position of the person involved; e) – the denomination, the amount and the value of the taken goods, also the manner that abuse consisted in[125].

Serious discontentments have also been reported when the Soviets have claimed that all the owners of goods taken from the Soviet Union during the war had to declare and to restore them. It was the question of the armament and the ammunition, above all, but it was also about any other goods produced both by Russian and Romanian factories from Bessarabia[126]. Even the objects from that region's churches had to be handed back. Of course, that disposition has been cause of abuses and conflicts, too, the persons that tried to elude this obligation being sanctioned according to the extremely severe stipulations of «the Law for the sabotage of the Armistice Convention»[127].

The hostility towards the Soviets has amplified due to some other abuses, too, such as the censorship the Romanian publications were subjected to. There was cut out even the newspaper «Tribuna Ardealului» which had appeared inclusively during the four years of Horthyst occupation. Thus, according to the stipulations of the Armistice Convention, the publishing, the bill sticking and the spreading of any publications of any kind that would contain excerpts meant to «perturb our relations with the United Nations» were forbidden[128]. Also, any theatrical or cinematographic performance that would have as a result, entirely or in some parts, the compromising of the good relations with the United Nations and especially with the Soviet Union[129]. On the basis of these stipulations, somehow vague, there have been made many abuses, being censored studies that had no political or historical subject (see appendix 2). Similar situation have existed also in the neighbouring countries. For example, in Hungary, a Soviet officer, that had the task of striking out the books about Horthy from the Library of the National Museum, had found a study from the XVII Century on *horticulture*. Because he did not understand what that book is about, he asked for that book to be destroyed, justifying that it made propaganda for Horthy[130]. In these circumstances, in the first part of December 1944, the reunion of the journalists from Cluj has taken place under the slogan «For the concord between the nationalities and friendship with the Soviet Union», in the building of the Central Advisory Committee of the National Democratic Front, in collaboration with the Romanian Democratic Union from the liberated Transylvania, where there have been analysed the new regulations imposed by the local and central authorities. At the meeting, there have been present, among other people, Hiuluba Emil, on the part of the General Command of the Stages, Teofil Vescan, representatives of the newspaper «Vilagossag», of a few newspapers from Bucharest, of the weekly publications «Plugarii» and «Erdely» and even a few representatives of «Tribuna Ardealului». It has been decided, at that reunion, that, in order to avoid the chauvinistic or «wrong» interpretations, every newspaper or publication would write in the first place on the «fascists» from every community and ethnic group and, at the same time, would systematically write articles on the cultural approaching between the Romanians and the Hungarians of Transylvania. In order to avoid, also, the publishing of some provocative articles, both in the Romanian and the Hungarian newspapers, it has been decided that an inter-journalistic commission would meet every week with the purpose of discussing the topical questions and deciding on the attitude the newspapers should have with regard to certain national problems that may come up in the future. During that meeting it has been discussed, also, about the role the newspapers can have in creating a favourable attitude towards the Soviet Union, abreast of the public opinion. Thus, according to the statements of some journalists that took part at the meeting, it was recommended for them to use in their rubrics, in order to strengthen the relations with the Soviet Union and for the thoroughly knowing of that country, excerpts from the newspapers of Bucharest that had reproductions and translations from Soviet writings, to use Russian bibliography, especially the Moscow editions of the Marx – Engels – Lenin Institute. At the same time, the journalists have delegated Hatos Romulus and Nagy Istvan to adhere to the Romanian Association for the strengthening of the relations with the Soviet Union (association that had its center in Bucharest, st. Dionisie, no.63), setting up, thus, a collaboration programme with the Soviet cultural circles. It has also been decided that the journalists of Cluj would proceed as soon as possible to the organization of a professional association, that would protect their interests before the employers[131]. The association's constitution meeting has taken place on the 20th of December 1944, in the presence of a large number of journalists. Matrai Ioan has been elected honorary chairman, Gheorghe V. Giurgiu – chairman and Balogh Edgard and Iacob Tis – vicepresidents[132].

Besides the censorship, the requisition of the radio sets from the population[133], also the totally unpopular measures imposed to the Romanian refugees, military or civilians, born in Bessarabia and northern Bukovina, were other reasons that caused discontentment and manifestations of hostility towards the Soviets. The statute of the citizens refugee from Bessarabia and Bukovina in Romania has been treated within the Armistice Convention as a separate problem, the Soviet Union showing an obvious interest for these persons, both in September 1944 and during the months to come. All the citizens that had been born or had lived in those provinces were compelled to return to their native territories, at the expense of the Romanian state. Thus, according to a note of the Allied Control Commission from December 1944, the Bessarabian refugees, including the members of their families that originated in Romanian territories that had never been part of Russia[134], were obliged to return to the Soviet Union. That measure has provoked real tragedies, many of them trying to escape from the forced return to U.S.S.R. by taking refuge from one locality to another or, in desperate cases, even by suicide[135].

There were several categories of citizens taken into account by the Soviet authorities. In the first place, there were the Bessarabians that came in Romania after the 22nd of June 1941 and that were, either they or their parents, subjects of the former Tsarist empire prior to the 7th of November 1917. Then, there were the inhabitants of northern Bukovina that came in Romania after the 22nd of June 1941. In the third place, there were the refugees and the persons that fled to Romania after the 22nd of June 1941, from any other region of the Soviet Union (Ukraine, Crimea, the Caucasus etc.)[136].

As for the rights of these inhabitants, the question of their consent has never been considered, on the contrary, on the entire Romanian territory it has been passed to an intense campaign of gathering data referring on these persons and on their transportation to the Soviet Union. Thus, conformable to an ordinance of the Ministry of Internal Affairs, the Special Service for the Allies Repatriated, from the 17th of November 1944, ordinance that has been transmitted also to the prefect's offices of northern Transylvania, there were specified the following:

- in order to hasten the measures of repatriating the Soviet citizens, there will be prescribed the payment of their pecuniary rights and the organization of their transportation;
- as soon as a number of at least 50 Soviet citizens enrolled for repatriation have received their pecuniary rights, their repatriation has to be accelerated;
- The General Board of the Romanian Railways should intervene so that all the requests for carriages or for special trains intended to transport the Soviet citizens would be guided only through the Special Service for Repatriations to U.S.S.R.;
- the transportations are to be supervised by the mandatory of the respective prefect's office, at the entraining stations, who would indite an official report in the presence of the Soviet mandatory etc.[137]

The action of «repatriating» the inhabitants of Bessarabia and Bukovina has intensified after the installation of the government of Dr. Petru Groza and especially after the drawing up of the decrees-laws regarding the regulation of the Romanian citizenship[138].

These are only some of the reasons that caused the breaking out of conflicts between the Soviets and Transylvania's inhabitants. Practically, of the vast problems of the relations between the Red Army's troops and the natives we have selected only a few aspects. The fact that the Romanian communist authorities and the Soviet authorities have done their best to hide the real deeds of some Soviet soldiers should not be overlooked. At the same time, beside the fact that not only northern Transylvania, but the entire Romanian territory had become an area from which «everything could be taken away»[139], there have been recorded throughout the country numerous cases of arresting, deportations, murders, rapes and many other abuses and humiliations. Similarly to the situation of the other Central-European countries (Hungary, Poland, Czechoslovakia, Germany)[140], the presence of the Soviet Army in Romania has given rise to a lot of hatred and will to revenge, instead of gratitude.

*

The withdrawal of the Romanian civil administration and the establishment of the Soviet supervised administration – in the framework of which incompetent and corrupt functionaries were many times appointed – has had baneful consequences in relation with many spheres, such as: the Law, the education, the medical system, the economic situation etc.

The Law was completely disorganized. The lack of judges and the keeping of the Hungarian legislation altogether with the Romanian one, introduced immediately after the liberation, have had as a consequence an even worse disorganization than the one existing in the administration. Each district guided itself upon different laws, the choice between them being most of the times imposed by the liking of the prefects or of the few judges. The courts were improvised, the same were the session houses. No sooner than December 1944, there have been drawn up a series of necessary rules referring to the civil jurisdiction, rules that started to be applied beginning with January 1945. Thus, the judicial system has been reorganized by creating 3-5 country courts in every district (in the district's capitals and in the main cities) and a tribunal, as a supreme instance. The principle of the one judge institution has been applied at the country courts, while at the tribunal there has been applied that of the panel of judges[141]. In a few districts – Năsăud, Cluj, Satu-Mare – there have been made some innovations in civil, penal, commercial and procedural matters. Thus, in case of dissension inside the panel of judges at the tribunal, a third judge was immediately assigned by the drawing of lots and the law suit was settled that very session. There was only by way of exception that a case could be tried within ten days.[142] Also, the trial of the contraventions has been organized on new basis, passing to the competence of the police judges. There was issued a penal warrant versus the contravener, warrant that could be contended with opposition only for innocence. The legal disputes were tried within 15 days by the instance that had issued the warrant and the sentence could be appealed only for reducing the penalties. The decisions could be contested within three days from the notifying in written form, at the notary of the locality where the defendant lived. The second decision of the court was executory, if the passed penalty was a pecuniary fee of up to 500 Pengö, while if the fee was bigger or if the delivered penalty was police jail or seizure of goods, the decisions of the appealing instance could be contested by appeal at the tribunal[143].

In the district of Mureş, unlike other districts, a series of transitory modifications had come into effect, a few rules referring to the civil jurisdiction, also a few procedural and organizing legal standards[144]. Thus, in Târgu-Mureş, Reghin, Miercurea Nirajului, Sângiorgiul de Pădure and Teaca were still functioning country courts. In Târgu-Mureş there were functioning the Tribunal and the Court of Appeal. The patrimonial law suits, that did not come within the Tribunal's competency, irrespective of their money value, were belonging to the country courts (provided, though, that the suit's value would not exceed 10.000 Pengö). The decisions of the country court's judges and of the Tribunal could be appealed only one time, following the procedure established by the law. The decisions of the Court of Appeal could not be contested. In case of need, the tribunal judges could deliberate their cases in the framework of the country courts, while the judges of appeal could deliberate at the Tribunal; also, within the Tribunal's senates, formed of the three members at the first instance, could be included those from the country courts. When appointing a time limit, the judicial instances were asked to take into account the difficulties of communication and transportation of the moment, so that the summoned ones would have enough time to come before the court. The mailing of the judicial dispositions or summons was forbidden. In the divorce suits, the presence of the persons or person that witnessed the civil marriage was not needed, as for the real estates, it was sufficiently if the sides presented certificates issued by the communal or urban cityhalls instead of the certificates issued by the public notaries[145].

During that period, two amnesties and pardons were afforded. On the 1st of February 1945, it has been forbidden the current pursuit and there have been pardoned the penalties of those convicted for illegal appropriation of objects and goods from the public institutions' patrimonies or from the missing or deported population, provided that these goods have been restored to the owners or have been placed at the disposal of the authorities, by any means. On the 6th of March 1945, the penalties for forest related trespassings have been pardoned and the current procedures have been suspended. The civil damage compensations have been reduced to a half[146].

It is noteworthy, at the same time, that after the 1st of February 1945, a period of persecution has begun, directed especially against the leaders and the members of the National Peasant Party and of the Greek Catholic community. For example, 14 intellectuals have been arrested in Oradea. Among these people, two of them – the Greek Catholic canon Gavrilă Stan, the rector of the Theological Academy and the lawyer Eugen Chiş – after being confined for many days, have been shifted to the Hungarian territory, without any notice on their part ever after. Dr. Dumitru Nacu has been arrested in Năsăud, former member of the parliament and prefect prior to 1940, refugee after the Vienna Award and returned home at the beginning of 1945. In Satu-Mare, there have been arrested Dr. Augustin Mircea, public notary and Dr. Virgil Codreanu, lawyer, while in Maramureş, the terror regime and the pressures against the Romanians have worsened, in order to force them to make statements favourable to the union of Maramureş with Ukraine[147].

*

At the same time, the inter-ethnic frictions, those between the Soviets and the natives, also the military developments have created perturbations in **the economic life** of the province. Many refugees, intellectuals, civil servants and artisans did not dare to return to their homes, as they still have had in mind, on one hand, the things that happened in 1940 and, on the other hand, as they were worried about the evolution of the situation in this province in the period that followed November 1944. Due to the general uncertainty, no process of rebuilding the economy could be initiated. Most of the financial institutions that had functioned during the war were then closed; four currencies were in circulation, simultaneously – lei, Pengö, Soviet Pengö and roubles – each district having a different exchange rate for them. The repairs could not be started due to the lack of materials and means of payment[148]. The entire economic life of the province was disorganized, partly because of the damages in the access ways. The roads, the bridges, the railways lines were almost impassable, even though some of them were partially rehabilitated through the labour of the population.[149] Due to that fact, the trade and the supplying were stagnating. Commodities such as the sugar, the salt, the soap, the oil etc. were almost nowhere to be found.[150] At the same time, the cereals and food crisis has been acutely felt in numerous regions, even though the main care in the economic sphere was the agriculture, which was most severely prejudiced both by the passing through of the battlefront and by the requisitions and the quotas imposed by the Soviets or by the robberies they have committed, all these having as a result a real dispossession of goods of the population. It was not about, as we have seen before, the allaying of some immediate needs, fact that could have been understood in the given war situation, but of robberies that have had serious negative consequences in the economic area.

Providing the food products was one of the main concerns of every prefect and mayor. However, despite the efforts that were made, the food providing had serious drawbacks. The number of domestic animals had considerably diminished, there was an acute lack of gas and seeds and most of the agricultural machineries were not functional.[151] At the prefect's office of the district of Mureş there were reaching reports of the mayors or of various inhabitants that pointed to the fact that the agricultural work could not be done, due to the lack of fuel, that in the regions where battles have taken place, the fields were still full of landmines and unexploded shells and that the indispensable goods, especially the flour, were lacking[152] . As for the transportation throughout the district, it has been done in satisfactory conditions, the bridges and the roads destroyed during the war being temporarily rehabilitated in the course of November, from wood.[153]

In the district of Cluj, also, the situation was serious. The food has become, by the beginning of the winter of 1944, almost inexistent. The bread, the meat, the vegetables, the sugar, the salt etc. were completely missing. It was possible to get by private bargain some products, but at enormous prices[154] . Also, the lack of firewood was so great that many families burnt their fences or some other things[155] . The prefect Teofil Vescan, at the beginning of December 1944, has asked the praetors from the areas around the former provisional border, by the ordinance no. 1154/1944, to form civil guards under the form of permanent patrols, which would obstruct the passing over «the borders» of the cattle, food and other goods.[156] It was the same prefect that tried, in order to provide a better supplying, to establish measures, by another ordinance from the 11th of December 1944, for the limitation of the speculation with milk, eggs, potatoes, meat, butter etc.[157] At the same time, during January 1945, the prefect has ordered the checking up of the butcher's shops, bakeries and other firms that marketed essential merchandises[158], fact that resulted in the finding that there were used exaggerated prices. In such conditions, the prefect's office has required that everything must be reverted to the set prices within three days , as for the merchants that refused to comply, their trade licenses were to be cancelled.[159]

In the district of Sălaj, a commission of inventory that carried on its activity in Şimleul Silvaniei, at the beginning of January 1945, pointed out to the deplorable state of the taverns and the shops of the town. The comodities were missing and the installations were destroyed. Part of the banks that had functioned during the whole war, were forced to suspend their activity in the autumn of 1944. For the merchants that had accounts in the now closed banks, it was impossible to continue their activities.[160] Numerous unlawful activities have also been recorded. The prefect's office of the district of Sălaj tried to provide, by various means, at least the most essential goods to the population. In order to prevent the exodus of these products to other districts (to the Szeckler's region, especially, where they could be sold at higher prices), the prefect was conditioning the giving of the trade licenses by the prior solving of the district market's requests.[161]

In the district of Bihor, the population was worried about the lack of essential commodities, especially of lamp oil, matches, salt etc. Due to the lack of lamp oil, the offices of the authorities closed at sunset, fact that displeased the population. In addition to that, due to the lack of means of conveyance, the shops could not be supplied, the post did not functioned in normal conditions and the phones could not be used but in two villages – regional capitals.[162]

A somewhat better situation existed in the district of Năsăud where, in the autumn of 1944, the villages have been mobilized for harvest or for sowing the land. There have been done agricultural labour even on the lands of the absent people, so that, through a series of measures of supplying and by forbidding the taking of the cereals out of the district, it was possible to pass quite easily the winter of 1944-

1945, providing both the population's demands and the obligations to supply the Red Army with 150 cereals freight cars. The diminution of the live stock has led to the regulation of the killing of animals. On the 1st of January 1945, the live stock inventory of the district was of 27.948 cattle, 839 horses, 76.025 sheep, 286 pigs and 15.700 fowls. Of these, 8900 cattle were given to the Soviet army. As the salt stock brought from Ocna Dejului has been consumed, in order to provide the population' s necessary of salt, it has been resorted to the district's salt deposits from Sărăţel and Dumitra, which have been put under strict surveillance. There have also been recorded difficulties in the supply with sugar, lamp oil, medicines and tobacco.[163]

Generally speaking, the crisis of the cereals, of the food products, of the medicines and of the fuel has been acutely experienced in many regions, while an eventual supplying from other districts of Romania was almost impossible due to the disorganized or destroyed ways of communication and to the chaos from the local and central administration. In fact, the severe economical condition of northern Transylvania and the removal of that territory from the Romanian state's administration has had negative consequences upon the entire economic situation of Romania. Thus – according to a statistic report from March 1945 (published in «Monitorul Oficial» and in the newspaper «Universul» – northern Transylvania had within the Romanian economy, an agricultural contribution of 1.303.002 hectares of tillable land, 1.074.466 hectares of hayfields and pastures, 577.693 hectares of orchards and vineyards and approximately 2.000.000 hectares of forest. The contribution in live stock was, in the same period, the following: horses – 285.000; cattle – 720.000; sheep – 1.679.000; goats – 97.000, pigs – 750.000; fowls – 4.500.000. The industrial contribution was: 720 industrial units, related to a country total of 3800, in the same period, with an invested capital of approximately 4 billions lei, given the country total of 52 billions lei. Of the industrial branches, the first place was held by the food industry, the wood industry and the metallurgic industry. Of the state industrial units, of a particular importance was the salt mill of Sighet, the Romanian Railways repair workshops from Cluj and the ironworks from Firiza de Jos. The forest patrimony of the liberated Transylvanian country, especially the wooded massives from Maramureş and Rodna, also the region from the Carpathians curvature (the districts of Ciuc, Odorhei and Trei-Scaune) represented a surface of approximately a third of the Romanian forest's total, prior to 1940 and as wood industry's operation, it was almost a half of the total. The mining patrimony comprised the mines of Baia-Mare, Baia-Sprie, Cavnic, Valea Roşie, Cărpiniş, Băiuţ and Rodna, the Ciuc and Odorhei regions, holding iron ores on a scale of 20 to 25 percent of the country's total; the iron pyrites of Rodna and Valea Vinului, with a smaller percentage of iron and more copper, besides the auriferous regions of Baia-Mare and Rodna-Veche. The leather industry was also well developed, representing 16 percent of the country's units total, 27 percent of the invested capital, 18 percent of the motive power and 32 percent of the number of the employees used in this branch in the entire country.[164]

The first workings of reconstruction in northern Transylvania have been those meant to rehabilitate the railroads, of a total length of 2.190 kilometers, that is a fifth of the entire country's railway network, as the first service that was set going and kept going with Romanian staff has been that of railway communications, thing that represented an important support for the military developments, both in various parts of Transylvania and in Hungarian territory, also in the Carpathians regions of Czechoslovakia and Poland.[165] At the beginning of December 1944, the railroad Cluj – Oradea has been rehabilitated and opened for traffic, the first passenger train that has resumed the connection between the two cities circulating the morning of the 7th of December, the drawing up of a trains timetable following on[166]. An increased attention has been payed to the postal and telephone service, too. In Cluj, a telephone manual central has been provisionally set up, also a few other telephone sets in the very beginning of November. Afterwards, telephone sets have been set up for all the civil authorities and for a number of approximately 100 private subscribers in the city[167] . In addition to that, there have been rehabilitated and restored to operations the postal offices of Sfântu-Gheorghe, Târgu-Secuiesc, Miercurea-Ciuc, Odorhei, Târgu-Mureş, Dej, Bistriţa, Zalău, Reghin.[168] We should not skip the fact that the serious economic problems of northern Transylvania have fed many times the tensions that existed between the local inhabitants. The epidemics, the famine, the poverty, the losses due to the military developments have contributed to the maintenance of an agitated state of affairs, marked by the rise of the danger of breaking out some violent incidents.

As for the health assistance and education systems, the situation was deplorable, the authorities being unable to handle the difficulties in these spheres.

The health assistance's situation was particularly severe. As a result of the German – Hungarian troops' withdrawal from northern Transylvania, which have taken when they departed all the sanitary materials and the medicines from the hospitals and the public protection institutions, from the private sanatoriums and drug stores, the civil population has remained without medical assistance.[169] The physicians were very few, most of the drug stores were closed, the medicaments were hard to find; with the exception of the Cluj district, there was no proper sanitary organization that could get through the drawbacks of that moment. On the 6th of November 1944, in Cluj it has been established a Medical College that has elected a provisional committee, led by dr. Elisabeta Constantinescu – Neuman, dr. Csogor Ludovic and dr. Liviu Telia, college that has functioned until the end of 1946.[170] To the malnutrition and the various diseases have also added the accidents caused by the landmines and the grenades from the areas where military operations have taken place, many wounded and mutilated persons could not be saved because of the lack of surgeons, dressings, prosthesis and other necessary things. Despite all the difficulties due to the lack of medicines, the physicians have started a campaign to prevent and remove the epidemics, especially the typhus, that made many victims. Unfortunately, the political interests began to show up in the health assistance sphere, too. Thus, in the district of Cluj, «The Commission for the purification of the Medical College» has started its activity, aiming to collect information about the political past of the physicians. The people that gave these informations had to send them in a signed and closed envelope, to the Municipal Sanitary Service's center, st. Vlahuţă, no. 1.[171] This fact has allowed the perpetration of many abuses, there have been created suspicions between well-known physicians, also between the medical personnel and the other categories of staff from the hospitals, thing that has had negative consequences on the functioning of the medical service.

As for the professors and the students of the faculty of medicine that fled to Sibiu in 1940, immediately after the liberation, they have manifested their will to return as soon as possible in northern Transylvania. By the end of October, Prof. Dr. Iuliu Haţieganu (the rector of the University of Cluj prior to the Vienna Award) has arrived in Cluj from Sibiu, at the head of a delegation of physicians, with the purpose of preparing the return of the students.[172] When they have arrived in Cluj, they were frightened of what they have seen. Their homes had been occupied, first by the Horthysts, then by the other «liberating» army.[173] In the war situation of those times, «Cluj was, in the autumn of 1944, a city in expectation, flooded by the lava of some alarming rumours»[174]. The return to Cluj had to be prepared on the fly. However, at the beginning of November 1944, Professor Iuliu Haţieganu has been replaced by Professor Alexandru Borza who came from Timişoara. Dean of the Faculty of Medecine was Professor Victor C. Papilian. The replacement of Haţieganu was not a normal one, as he was arrested in fact the same month[175]. The Professor Ioan Goia has had an important role in the taking of Professor Haţieganu out of the imprisonment of the Sibiu's police. In that late autumn of 1944, he has «run» to every local authorities and, depending on the moment and on the person he spoke to, he showed who was the arrested professor and how much did he do for the students. Also, Goia has threatened the people that kept the professor in arrest that they would be responsible for his condition, as he was suffering from diabetes and had polyallergy, too. Iuliu Haţieganu has been taken out of the arrest and moved for three months in a side-room of the Medical Clinic (that he had formerly led), under military surveillance. The sister nuns Andreea and Ştefania Silaghi took care of him.[176] The Professor Iuliu Haţieganu's incrimination should not have been a surprise in the Romanian political climate of the period from 1944 to 1945. Restored to his professorship after that sad moment, Professor Haţieganu resisted until 1948, when Professor Aurel Moga has accepted to collaborate for his «master»'s elimination from the university.[177]

Because of the events that have taken place in northern Transylvania after the liberation, it was only after the reestablishment of the Romanian administration in this territory that a large part of the fled professors and students have returned. In the summer of 1945, the administrative and the technical department of the University have returned and, at the same time with the University, the Faculty of Medicine has returned, too.

As for **the education** field, the first concern of the authorities was that of restoring the elementary schools to functioning conditions. These schools were confronted with enormous difficulties, due to the lack of teachers and schoolmen, of buildings and didactic materials etc. Also, the situation in northern Transylvania was far more complex and complicated than the rest of the country, because the Hungarian regime of the 1940 – 1944 period has suppressed almost completely the education in Romanian language. After the liberation, it could be hardly organized at all a reasonable number of elementary schools, and that happened mostly with the aid of the local inhabitants that have repaired the buildings and have contributed to the achievement of a summary didactic material. Despite all those efforts, in most of the northern Transylvanian districts, the recommencing of the courses has succeeded no sooner than December 1944.[178]

In Sălaj, not all of the elementary schools were opened even in March 1945. That situation was due both to the deteriorations occured during the war or to the occupation of the school buildings by Romanian and Soviet military units and to the lack of the teaching staff. For instance, the state civil girls school of Zalău has resumed its activity not earlier than the 2nd of January 1945. Of the six teachers of the school, only two of them were trained. The inferior agricultural school from Şimleul Silvaniei has not functioned at all during the school year 1944 – 1945.[179]

In the district of Năsăud, the School Inspectorate has asked on the 24th of November 1944 for the support of the prefect's office for the beginning of the scool year. In this purpose, it has been required the effectuation of a census of the children from 7 to 14 years old in absolutely all the localities (census that would specify the sex of the children, their ethnic and confessional origin), also to be made a situation with the teachers and the schoolmen and in the localities where there were no teachers, male teachers from the neighbouring villages were to be sent.[180] In addition to that, the Inspectorate has asked the prefect's office to involve in the cleaning of the schools buildings and in supplying with firewood and to command the immediate starting of the school where teaching staff was available.[181] The next day, the prefect has sent in every district's village a note that contained the following: «...the elementary education has not started under the pretext that the school building could not be rehabilitated or that there was no inventory etc., nothing is being done, while with goodwill and a bit of energy it could have been arranged in each village a buiding and, if not a schoolman, at least the village's priest could have been taken care of the village's children two or three hours a day. Everybody is waiting for everything to be given to them in readiness, few people understand the exceedingly hard times and give their necessary support. I ask you to command that within 8 days, the elementary education to be resumed in every village, otherwise the mayors, the secretaries, the teachers and even the priests will be held responsible»[182]. It seems that, as a result of the prefect's note, in many villages it has been responded in a positive manner, because during December on the prefect's office address there have reached several confirmations that the school year has started or could be started in a few days. Thus, on the 11th of December, the praetor's office of the region Rodna has sent to the prefect's office the following address: «...the elementary education has started in all the elementary schools from Rodna region, the schools have been arranged by the inhabitants of the villages and supplied with the needed firewood»[183]. In the district of Năsăud, more than in the other northern Transylvanian districts, through the local inhabitants contribution, there have been repaired the school buildings and it has been improvised a summary didactic material instead of the destroyed one. During December 1944, the beginning of the courses has succeeded in most of the elementary schools and kindergartens, using 292 teachers and 153 schoolmistresses. Also, in every elementary school, there were organized special classes for the instruction of the pupils that had to take their additional examinations. 320 pupils from the districts of Someş, Maramureş and Mureş, also, have attended these classes.[184]

In the great cities, populated mainly by Hungarians, they have kept their schools organized by themselves, the Romanians having but a few school buildings by the end of 1944 and the beginning of 1945. For example, in Târgu-Mureş, out of nine secondary schools, only one was reserved to the education in Romanian language.[185] In some villages from Mureş, due to the lack of school buildings, the classes have taken place in private houses, that were many times in an advanced state of decay.[186] In Cluj, the schools have been opened by the end of 1944, too. The Hungarian pupils could begin the school year in the former school buildings of the state and in the buildings of the confessional schools, while for the education in Romanian language there have been opened the buildings of the Highschool «George Bari]iu», of the normal school for boys and of the Highschool «Principesa Ileana».[187] In these buildings, three secondary schools have functioned, with a very large number of students, that could have been enough for six schools. That fact has had a negative impact because of the agglomeration that existed within the schools and the boarding schools. In the city of Cluj, there have been opened two boarding schools for Romanian pupils. The Greek Catholic deaconry's boarding school has been opened on the 22nd of November 1944 for the pupils of the «George Bariţiu» Highschool[188] and the Romanian Orthodox Episcopate from Cluj has announced that on the 1st of December would open the girls boarding school in Avram Iancu street and the one for boys in Malinovsky Square.[189]

The conditions imposed to the pupils in order to obtain a place in the boarding schools were pretty much unbearable for many families, given those times situation. The Orthodox Diocese required the pupils to pay an advance of 3000 Pengö (90000 lei) and bring an initial stock of food products, which would mean 15 kgs of bread flour, 3 kgs of flour, 0,3 kg of corn flour, 1 kg of cheese, 30 eggs, 1 kg jam, 20 kgs potatoes, 5 kgs of onions, 10 kgs of cabbage, 3 kgs of beans, 2 kgs of lard, 1 litre of oil, 10 kgs of vegetables.[190] At the boarding school of the Bariţiu Highschool, every pupil had to bring, beside the payment of the study and accomodation taxes, the following food products:60 kgs of bread flour, 10 kgs of flour, 5 kgs of lard, 5 litres of sunflower oil, 100 eggs and two kitchen towels. Of all these, at the beginning of the school year, the pupils had to pay 400 Pengö (12000 lei) and when they enter the boarding school, they had to bring 20 kgs bread flour, 1 litre sunflower oil, 50 eggs and a kitchen towel.[191] In addition to these, the pupils also had to bring a table cloth that was supposed to be given back at the end of the school year, bedclothes (two blankets or eiderdowns, a pillow, two pillow cases and two bed sheets) and mattresses. At the same time, the pupils were informed by the boarding school's administration that the latter reserves itself the right to increase or to diminish the taxes during the school year, according to the evolution of the market.[192]

As for the university education, the city's Hungarian university has been moved to Szombathely, with the withdrawal of the German – Hungarian forces from Cluj. However, a few Hungarian teachers native from northern Transylvania have stayed. They affirmed that they represented the Hungarian University of Cluj and that they wanted to resume the courses, and they did, but without a sufficient number of students and professors.[193]

On the 13th of January 1945, by the ordinance no. 413/1945, the following measures have been taken:

1 – the suspension of the university autonomy;

2 – the abolition of the self-leading of the Academy of Agriculture and its integration as a separate faculty within the University. It was ensured the observance of the staff's rights, in relation with those of the persons from the University;

3 – the dissolution of the University's Senate;

4 – on the basis of the equality of rights between nations, it has been given the order: a – on the basis of the continuity by right, the Hungarian University of Cluj would proceed its activity in the future, according to the decisions of the above mentioned ordinance; b – the Romanian University would start its activity;

5 – the settlement of the problems related to the well functioning of the universities, to the assignment and the allocation of the buildings to be used etc. was the competence of a joint commission formed of three mandatory members from each of the two universities;

6 – the university senates had the duty to prescribe all the measures, calls and appointments;

7 – the university senates had the duty to organize the universities on a democratic and people's basis;

8 – after the reorganization of the universities, the provisional Senates were to resign and the universities, regaining their autonomy, were to elect new Senates etc.[194]

The decision of the Cluj prefect's office to allow the two university to function has provoked strong protests on the part of many citizens of Romanian ethnic origin from the city, fact that determined the issue of a new ordinance by means of which the application of the first ordinance has been postponed, until the 10th of February 1945. Also, the intervention of the prefect in the internal organization of the universities has called forth the protests of the teaching staff from the two higher education establishments.[195]

Generally speaking, the population's and even the authorities' efforts to provide the running of the school system have also been thwarted by the dissatisfaction existing among the few teachers that worked back then, dissatisfactions related to the fact that the wages were very small and were given many times with delay. Also, the teachers were frequently asked to perform various administrative workings.[196] In addition to these, the same as it happened with the physicians, too, there were beginning to appear among the teachers suspicions, purifications and interethnic conflicts.

By the end of November 1944, it has been created the Commission for the purification of the Secondary and Elementary Teaching Staff from Cluj, that took the following decisions: 1 – to vigilantly investigate all the past of all the members of the teaching staff, taking into account especially the fascist or democratic attitude of the teachers and schoolmen and to inform about the wrong and prejudicial attitudes, past and present of the teaching staff's members; 2 – to suggest the authorities the removal from the school's leaderships of all the principals that have served the former regime after the 19th – 20th of March 1944, the possibility to remain to their chairs was to be considered only if there was an acute crisis of teaching staff and there were no special objections with regard to their behaviour.[197] The ones that were required to come before the commission for purification have been summoned for the first time on the 14th of December 1944, being decided, at the same time, that the commission's resolutions could be appealed at the Commission for Verification the Commission for Purification about the Central Committee of the National Democratic Front, in collaboration with the Romanian Democratic Union from Cluj. The ones that refused to come before the commission were forbidden to profess any longer and were to be pursued for sabotage, together with the principals of the schools were they had worked.[198]

In addition to the pressures exerted upon the teaching staff on the part of the leftist groups, the interethnic conflicts have also been felt within the education institutions. They have increased especially after the return of the Romanian refugees who could no longer occupy the teaching positions that they had before august 1940, because, in the meantime, Hungarian teachers and schoolmen had been appointed, so that they could not be removed.[199]

However, despite all the economic difficulties and the social and political instability of those times, in the northern Transylvanian great cities various other education or cultural institutions have resumed their activity or have been established. Thus, in Cluj on the 30th of November 1944, by a prefect's ordinance, it has been established the Institute for mining prospecting and research, the main purpose of which was the organization, the prospecting and the exploitation of the northern Transylvanian mine's wealth, that is petroleum, methane gas, salt, bauxite and gold.[200] In the same period of time, the Theatre and the Romanian Opera House of Cluj have resumed their activities[201], and at the end of December, the Institute of French Studies has been reopened, placing at the public's disposal the library within its building[202].

*

In northern Transylvania and especially in the Cluj region, **the confrontations of ethnic nature and the social and economical problems have been doubled by the political ones**. Immediately after the liberation, the Regional Committee of the Romanian Communist Party (P.C.R.) organized in Cluj its center, the authority of which has covered the entire Transylvania. Gradually, with the advance of the Soviet forces in Transylvania, it has been noticed an intense extension of the communist network. Thus, it has come up to the point where in every district capital would function a municipal organization of the P.C.R. (the structures of which were meant to control the whole public life) and also organizations in every small region.[203] There have also been created the so-called «party cells», formed of the communists from the education institutions, factories, hospitals, post and railways, the street committees, too, that had an important role in the identification of the political enemies and in the organization of propaganda actions. The main task of every district committee was to recruit in a very short period of time as many members as possible, irrespective of their ethnic origin or their political past.[204] The adhering in a large number of the Jews and especially of the Hungarians to the P.C.R. has created acute manifestations of hostility in the region on the part of the Romanians and that happened the more so as the members of the party organizations from the countryside made an intense propaganda among the local inhabitants in order to determine them to adhere to the Communist Party or to other leftist parties and organizations, using a series of means of compulsion. There were situations when the communists have seized the oil presses, the mills, the boilers for brandy (*ţuică*) etc., so that the peasants were allowed in only if they subscribe to the Communist Party. Those who refused were constrained to bear a series of cavils, the services to them being delayed as much as possible.[205] We mention two situations for exemplification. On the 19th of February 1945, at the Police Inspectorate of Cluj has reached a report that specified that during the last few weeks, the members of the leftist organizations made an intense propaganda among the peasants, in order to determine them to adhere to F.N.D., making use of the following means: 1) the members of that organization were controlling the peasant mills, the oil presses and the woolcards, so that the peasants were forced to adhere to the leftist parties, while the ones that refused had to wait for two or three weeks and, many times, as they were exasperated, they accepted to join those organizations; 2) simultaneously with these actions, it was being made propaganda among the peasants referring to the agrarian reform and by the endowering of the communist organizations with agricultural machineries, offered by the Soviet Union.[206] On the 26th of February 1945, a peasant from the village of Jucu de Jos (district of Cluj), former liberal, affirmed that in his village and in the neighbouring villages «some Jews gentlemens and dandies are walking by, followed by Russian soldiers, telling us that we are all the same if we adhere to the democrats, in the Democracy's Front and, because this call did not work, they have sent us to the notary's offices and served out wheat at a price of 28 Pengö (840 lei) per bushel, but only for those who adhere, while those who do not enroll for the democrat's lists get nothing or if they give wheat to any of them, they give it for the price of 56 Pengö, that is exactly double. Because there are still very few Romanians that enter their names, these agents threaten that the ones who do not enter their names will be deported in Siberia. The things mentioned above happen also among the peasants of Gădălin, Răscruci, Feiurd and Popeşti»[207].

The fact that the Communist Party, together with its allies, wanted to get the power was not something new. They have expressed that request even from the first resignation of the Sănătescu government. Their failure has been due mainly to the King who has entrusted the formation of the government, both in November and in December 1944, to a general. Anyway, beginning with January 1945, the pressure of the F.N.D. has intensified, as it was supported by the Soviet Union, of course.

On the 24th of January 1945, it has taken place the meeting of the F.N.D.'s Council, regarding the discussions from Moscow, the essence of which had been the overthrowing of the Rădescu government. The discussions were also centered round the F.N.D.'s programme that was to be applied the moment they take over the power.[208] Related to the problem of Transylvania, the shorthand record of the meeting bring up the following: «...Transylvania, until this moment, due to Maniu and to the political circles that support him, has not been returned completely to Romania», but, drawing a parallel to the F.N.D's programme, Gheorghiu-Dej has affirmed that «we must show that this type of politics would bring back our prisoners that still are in the U.S.S.R. and, by doing this, we mobilize their families to join us; they would give us back northern Transylvania and, through this fact, we mobilize the Transylvanians, showing them why we did not have it back yet and, finally, showing all the improvements that a F.N.D. government would bring to the country»[209].

On a brief analysis of this document, we notice, beside the intention of taking over the government by the F.N.D., that Transylvania had become, as Brătianu has affirmed, not only a means for blackmail, but also a precious political capital for the leftist parties.

On the 31st of January, another F.N.D.'s meeting took place, followed by others that have been organized as the succession of events accelerated. The promise obtained from Moscow that Transylvania will be restored entirely to Romania has provided the Romanian communists a strong trump, that they have skilfully used in the struggle for taking hold of the power. As a matter of fact, the establishment of the Romanian administration in northern Transylvania on the 9th of March, that is three days after the installation of the government Petru Groza, was not only a political and administrative measure but especially a psychological element, meant to provide credibility to a preponderantly leftist government.

If the tactics of attracting the minorities was successful, it was not the same with the communist propaganda among the Romanian population. The adhering in a large number of the Jews and especially of the Hungarians to P.C.R. has provoked manifestations of hostility on the part of the Romanians, that went from the passive discontentment of the majority to a few acute manifestations. In fact, the very ethnic belonging of the communist party's members from the region explains very well a phenomenon that Moscow thought to be one of rejection by the Romanians of the idea to become members of the communist party. The communism was considered by the Romanians to be an expression of the Russian expansionism and the adhering of Transylvania's Hungarian minority to that party did nothing but to consolidate the assumption of the existence of an occult Russian – Hungarian conspiracy which was trying to destroy Romania, under the red flag of the communism.[210]

The fact that the Hungarians were the first that hurried to adhere to that party, in an attempt not necessarily unnatural to line politically to the conqueror's position, has made nothing but to embitter the Romanian's opposition and to provoke, beside the few acute incidents, a state of general discontentment.

The settlement of the national problem (the ceasing of the interethnic incidents), too, has been one of the priorities of the northern Transylvanian communist leaders, especially because of the interest that Moscow showed to that province. Thus, in the communist party's publications (especially in the newspaper «Scânteia») and also on the occasion of various manifestations, the communist leaders have started a campaign the burden of which was that of forgetting the excesses of the previous period and the settlement of an understanding between all the ethnic communities. It has come up to the cutting out of the judicial term of ***minority***, in December 1944, and its replacement with the expression ***coinhabiting nationalities***. That change of terminology has been decreed in Bucharest, during the Rădescu government. It has materialized, in fact, within the entire country's territory only in the summer of 1945. In northern Transylvania, the official reports of the police and gendarmerie inspectorates, of the townhalls etc. have used only the term ***minority***.[211]

The most often found forms of resistance to communism were the actions of the «historical» parties and, first of all, of the National Peasant Party (P.N.T.), that carried on a propaganda hostile to the Soviet Union and to the regime that was about to install in the country.[212] Then, the Soviet authorities have struck against the groups and the more or less secret societies[213], organized by young intellectuals or by a series of volunteer officers that had fought in the eastern battlefront. These groups (many times in close connection with P.N.T) manifested their hostility towards the Soviets and the communists. It is interesting, in this regard, a «report – résumé» drawn up in the summer of 1945 by the Cluj police on the political activity of the «reactionaries», in fact, on the activity of P.N.T. during the Soviet administration: «...The National Peasant Party – the Maniu's group – is a strong ironguardist organization that carries on an intense opposition and propaganda. Their meeting places are the Romanian – Orthodox Theology, the normal school from Roma street, the office of the lawyer Justian Blaga, the office of the lawyer Aurel Stănescu, Mihai Viteazul Square (on market days being the meeting place with the villages representatives). The leaders of the Manist group are: professor Emil Haţegan, the lawyers dr. Aurel Stănescu, dr. Aurel Socol, dr. Eugen Olteanu, dr. Emil Blaga, the Romanian Orthodox priest Miron Pop, the bishop dr. Nicolae Colan, Aurel Coza (former general inspector), the lawyer Romul Pop, dr. Tiberiu Rebreanu and the priest Forma. The Manist group carries on propaganda among the Romanians, requesting the evacuation of the Hungarian element from Transylvania under the form of an exchange of population and also the evacuation of the Russian communist elements... The most active propagandists are the priests and the countryside's teachers...»[214]

Few days after the withdrawal of the Romanian administration from northern Transylvania, on the 17th of November, in Cluj, the forming meeting of the Romanian Democratic Union from the Liberated Transylvania (U.D.R.A.E.) has taken place, in the presence of a pretty large number of Romanians, belonging to every professional categories and also the representatives of the two Romanian religions.[215] It was the first Romanian political manifestations since the Cluj's liberation. The organization's honorary president was Emil Haţieganu, executive president was prof. Aurel Coza, secretary – Gheorghe Giurgiu, chief editor of «Tribuna Ardealului»[216]. The formation of the Union has been welcome by the representatives of all the parties and political groups, its members insisting on the proportional representation of every nationality of Transylvania in the public positions. Aurel Coza contended, however, that he understands that representativeness not on the basis of the situation of the autumn of 1944, when there were over 250.000 refugees and over 150.000 deported Jews, but on the basis of the situation prior to the 30th of August 1940.[217] The U.D.R.A.E., that has proposed for itself as a main goal «to struggle against the fascism wherever he might be camouflaged», did not have a very sound presence, being put into shade by the political parties' actions. Actually, after the return of the Romanian administration in northern Transylvania, the organization has ceased its activity, many of its members becoming active presences in various other organizations.[218]

In analysing the persons that have opposed to the ascent of the communism, we can affirm that, from the point of view of the social and professional structure of the Romanian population, the intellectuals, the peasants and the officers (that have fought in the East in the framework of the Romanian Army or that have been fled for four years in the free Romanian territories) have organized the most important actions of resistance and protest, actions that began to be recorded with anxiety by the local and district's police inspectorates. Thus, in the region of Năsăud, it has been identified the organization «Haiducii lui Avram Iancu»[219] (Avram Iancu's outlaws), that has distinguished itself by a vast action of spreading anti-Russians leaflets. Another organization has been «Societatea Patrioţilor»[220] (the Society of Patriots), a secret military organization that was pursuing the installation of a government formed mainly of National Peasant Party's representatives. Referring to this organization, representatives of the Soviet power drew the attention to the fact that it was very extended, among its leaders there were active members of the Romanian General Headquarters and it had a large support on the Army's part. Simultaneously with the organization of such societies, the Romanian intellectuals and officers had connections with members of the Western legations from Romania and they were spreading not only in northern Transylvania, but in the whole country, maps with the inter-war Romanian territory and with the royal marks.[221]

Actually, prior to the installation of the Petru Groza government, the propaganda actions of the communists and their sympathizers from northern Transylvania did not have much of an echo, as they represented especially a Hungarian – Jewish minority. The number of the P.C.R. members by the end of 1944 was 1000 persons. The Ploughmen's Front did not had a bigger success, either. The findings of that period are almost identical with the findings referring to the communists, with the only difference that the Ploughmen's Front has operated especially in the countryside, carrying on a propaganda connected to the agrarian question, while the communist party has done it among the urban workers.[222] In fact, the majority of the political left's actions from the countryside have had a pretty limited nature in that period, because of the strong influence of the National Peasant Party.

*

At the same time, under the cover of the Soviet domination, a series of secessionist actions have been encouraged. Thus, in **Maramureş**, Ukrainean communist elements, infiltrated with the Moscow's hidden support, have tried to remove the Romanian authority and to annex the Maramureş's territory to Ukraine.

Immediately after the 23rd of August 1944, a few leaders of the Romanians from Maramureş have been imprisoned by the Hungarian authorities. In prison, they have formed a Romanian National Council, a structure that was to take over the district's leadership immediately after the liberation. A committec has been elected, formed of 20 members, the president elected being prof. I. Bilţiu Dăncuş.[223] When the Soviet Army has entered the district, on the 18th of October 1944, the Soviet commander, col.Ghiomin has asked Moscow by radio for instructions regarding the statute of Maramures. Having confirmed that this region was part of Romania, the Soviet commander has given the leadership of the district to the Romanian National Council (S.N.R.).[224] On the 1st of November 1944, units of the Romanian gendarmes legions have entered the city of Sighet, units that have been welcome by the Romanian intellectuals that had left in the ceded territory and by the Romanian authorities established for the administration of the city. They have offered their support for the installation and the well dcvelopment of the police structures, both from the point of view of the state security and of the public order and peace, in a situation where the Romanian inhabitants were discontented by the injustices done to them both during the Hungarian administration and after its removal.[225] Once they were installed in the territory, the gendarmes formations have started their police activity, by organizing auxiliary civil guards that had the main charge of protecting the citizen's lifes and wealth, that have became a prey for the robbers.[226]

In the meantime, in the Maramureş regions from the right side of the river Tisa, an effervescent action of annexation of the sub-Carpathian Ukraine to the Soviet Ukraine has intensified. On the 24th of November, a people's meeting took place in Muncaci, where it has been decided the accomplishment of this Ukraineans' desideratum.[227] The influence of this annexation has been immediately felt on the left side of Tisa, too, in the district of Maramureş, especially in the city of Sighet and in the villages with Ukrainean population, where there have appeared the promoters of the idea of the union between the whole Maramureş with Ukraine.[228] The entire period from the liberation of northern Transylvania to the reinstallation of the Romanian administration in March 1945 has been exploited by the Ukrainean communists from Maramureş who tried to determine a campaign for the annexation of this territory to the Soviet Union.[229] This propaganda has been done in the beginning in a masked manner, in various forms, then it has been manifested openly, making use of the cooperating elements from the region, recruited by agents of the Ukrainean secret police. They have come into contact both with the Soviet authorities in the area, and especially with the Ukrainean nationalists that embraced this cause.[230] The position of the Maramureş's Jews and Hungarians with regard to the eventual annexation of that territory to Ukraine and, implicitly, to the Soviet Union, was ambiguous, as that was considered by them to be a better thing than the return to Romania; obviously, the solution preferred by these minorities would have been the annexation to Hungary or the constitution of an independent Transylvania.[231]

The Ukraineans leaders have addressed a message to Stalin and to N. Hrusciov!!!, the leader of the Soviet Ukraine, by means of which they required the annexation of Maramureş to the Soviet Union. At the beginning of 1945, S.N.R. existed rather formally, the power being actually exerted by the Ukrainean civil servants, strongly implicated in the administrative structures. They have put many pressures on the population, from generous offers in exchange for the support to the annexation of Maramureş to Ukraine up to threatenings with the destructions of the goods, deportation in Siberia or extermination.[232] In the same period of time, at the Soviet's request, the gendarmes legion instated in the district in November has been withdrawn, first in Zalău, then in the southern part of the district of Bihor. That fact has favoured even more the actions of the secessionists, which have culminated with a meeting for annexing Maramureş to Ukraine, organized in Sighet, on the 20th of January 1945. The result of these actions has been the election, by the end of January 1945, of a city council formed of 32 members (mainly Ukraineans and Hungarians).[233] The former Romanian functionaries have been dismissed. In the beginning of February 1945, the Ukraineans have organized new secessionist activities, that have reached a climax in a meeting in the course of which a district council has been elected, that was supposed to take care of the «settlement» of the Maramureş's internal problems. On the same occasion, it has been decided: a) – the introduction of the Ukrainean language in the administration (ignoring thus the existence of the Romanian and Hungarian population)[234]; b) – setting an exchange rate for the roubles and the pengö issued by the Soviet Army; c) – the opening of Ukrainean schools; d) – the compulsoriness for the Romanian and Hungarian schools to introduce six hours of Ukrainean language in their weekly studies programmes; e) – the adoption of the Maramureş official flag – red, with the hammer and the sickle, having written on it the slogan «Long live the union of Maramureş with the Soviet Ukraine» etc. By the end of February, this new district council has decreed the seizure of the fled Germans and Hungarians' properties and the compulsoriness for the Romanians to work together with the Soviet soldiers at the rehabilitation of the communication ways.[235] Also, beginning with December 1944 and especially in January 1945, in the entire district the radio sets have been taken from the population. Thus, the possibility to inform was almost inexistent. From Romania there were no newspapers to reach the district, due to the lack of transportations means, the news being collected from the people coming from the Old Kingdom, from northern Transylvania or from Hungary.[236] There were a few official information to be found in the rather poor local press, «Maramuresul», newspaper of the S.N.R. from Maramureş, the first number of which has appeared on the 10th of Dccember 1944 and «Poporul», a newspaper with articles written both in Romanian and Hungarian, that appeared since the 23rd of December 1944. The latter newspaper has replaced, in fact, the communist newspaper «Lumina poporului», that suspended its activity on the 6th of December 1944.[237]

Given the situation created in Maramureş, the reaction of the Romanian leaders from Bucharest and from Maramureş was not waited too long. The leaders of the Romanians from Maramureş have decided to convoke a meeting in the framework of which the population would decide the future of Maramureş. The meeting was to take place on the 5th of March 1945, but the Soviet High Command, at the request of the secessionist Ukraineans, has forbidden the development of any Romanian action. Due to that situation and in order to avoid the starting of some bloody incidents, the Romanian leaders have decided to countermand the meeting, though numerous incidents and provocations have been reported.[238]

We must make mention of the fact that the anti-Romanian attitude of the Ukraineans was favoured not only by the Moscow's support, but also by the fact that, geographically, Maramureş is a region isolated from the rest of Romania (due to its mountains of more than 2000 meters and the destruction of the few railways and roads that made the connection with the rest of Romania's territory)[239], its administration being formed inclusively of Ukrainean elements that did not know or did not speak Romanian on purpose, thing that had given rise to acute discontentments and tensions among the Romanian inhabitants.

The restoration of the former Sub-Carpathian Ukraine, the frontiers of which would have expanded up to the south of the city of Baia-Mare, has been discussed in Czechoslovakia, too. That happened the more so as prior to December 1944 no Czechoslovakian authority has arrived in the territory, so that the Ruthenian population, influenced by the Soviet officers' propaganda related to the establishment of the Sub-Carpathian Ukraine, has set about to robberies and atrocities against the population of a different ethnic origin, especially the Hungarians.[240]

However, despite the secessionist actions of the Ukraineans, one month after the installation at Bucharest of the communist government of dr. Petru Groza, on the 9th of April 1945, in Maramureş, too, the Romanian administration has been reinstated. The same day, the Czechoslovakian government «surrendered» the Transcarpathian Ukraine to the Soviets. As a result of that decision, the Romanian government has tried (without success) to conclude an agreement with the Soviet Union on the exchange of Romanian population from the Transcarpathian Ukraine with the Ukraineans from Maramureş and the bringing in Romania of the churches and of the Romanian religious objects existing there.[241]

As for the tensions between the Romanians and the Ukraineans, they have not been settled even after the introduction of the Romanian civil administration in the region. Several cases of frontier trespassing and thefts were reported, the victims of which were Romanian inhabitants mostly. For example, on the 28th of June 1945, ten persons wearing Soviet military uniforms have appeared within the radius of the village Borşa (district of Maramureş). They have arrested six shepherds together with their flock, disappearing afterwards with the whole prey on the other side of the frontier. Those shepherds have never returned home.[242]

NOTES:

[1] Florin Constantiniu, «*O istorie sincera...*», pp 448

[2] Claudiu Porumbăceanu, *op. cit.*, pp 87

[3] Constantin Hlihor, Ioan Scurtu, *op. cit.*

[4] «*Tribuna*», the 17-23 of October 1991, pp 7

[5] Nicolae Ciachir, *op. cit.*, pp 330

[6] «*Istoria P.C.R.*», Synthesis VI, pp 272

[7] *Ibidem*, pp 273

[8] *Ibidem*, pp 273

[9] Titus Podea, «*Transilvania*», ed. Fundaţiei Culturale Române, Bucharest, pp 228

[10] *Ibidem.*

[11] «*23 August 1944. Documente 1944 – 1945*», vol.III, Ed. Ştiinţifică şi Enciclopedică, Bucharest, 1985, doc. 1013

[12] *Ibidem*, doc. 1014

[13] «*23 August. Documente*», doc. no. 1017

[14] A.N.R.Cluj, Fund «*Biroul de Cenzură Cluj-Turda*», the 12th of November 1944, «...the government has released an official statement in the newspapers of Sunday, the 12th of November 1944, by means of which it announced the Romanian people that in northern Transylvania the Romanian administration is being gradually established and that, of the 11 districts, in 5-6 of them the Romanian administration has already been established. This government communique is good for children and for nannies. Nothing is true. In the first place, the Ministry of Internal Affairs did not know what is happening in the country. It is not even known if the alleged establishment of the administration has been done in 5 or 6 districts. Are we, the simple citizens, supposed to know that thing?... The Romanian gendarmerie has been driven away from Someşeni. From Târgu-Mureş, all the recently installed Romanian authorities

have been removed. The same in Szekler's Sfântu-Gheorghe. From Zalău and Şimleul Silvaniei, also. The police and the volunteers detachment awaiting in Feleac has got the categorical command to leave the village at once, from a captain, and that happened in a territory under Romanian sovereignty. We have been informed that it was given today the order that all the authorities of the Romanian state and even the solitary functionaries that came as a result of the Bucharest government's order are to leave the territory of northern Transylvania in 24 hours. It is also being spoken about a general command that would be billed in the districts of northern Transylvania, which prescribes that all those who came in that territory after the 11th of October must leave it within 48 hours, under very severe sanctions...»

[15] «*Dreptatea*», year II, series 2, no.127, the 28th of January 1945, pp 2

[16] «*23 August. Documente*», doc. no. 1029

[17] «*Dreptatea*», the 28th of January 1945, pp 2

[18] Valeriu Florin Dobrescu, «*România şi organizarea postbelică a lumii...*», pp 73

[19] *Ibidem.*

[20] Gh. Onisoru, «*Statutul Transilvaniei...*», pp 421

[21] A.M.A.E., D. Transilvania/1944-1945, vol. 139 C.A.C., f.207-212

[22] *Ibidem*, pp 211

[23] A.N.R.B-ţa, Fund «*Prefectura Judeţului Năsăud*», Dossier 48/1944

[24] A.N.R.Cluj, Fund «*Inspectoratul de Poliţie Cluj*», Dossier 159/1944 and A.N.R.B-ţa, *Fund cit.*, Dossier 48/1944

[25] A.N.R.B-ţa, Fund «*Gustav Zikeli, 1876 – 1952, Autobiografie*», Bistriţa, 1951, pp 67

[26] A.N.R.Ms, Fund «*Prefectura Judeţului Mureş*», Dossier 24/1945

[27] Ioan Mureşan, «*Situaţia social-politică şi economică a judeţului Năsăud în timpul administraţiei militare sovietice (13 octombrie 1944 – 12 aprilie 1945)*», in «Revista Bistriţei», VII, The district's Museum Bistriţa Năsăud, Casa Editorială şi de Presă Glasul Bucovinei, Iaşi – Rădăuţi, 1993, pp 264; Ştefan I. Pop, «*O pagină de istorie. Viaţa judeţului Năsăud de la 13 octombrie 1944 la 13 martie 1945*», Tipografia Minerva, Bistriţa, 1947, pp 16

[28] A.N.R.B-ţa, Fund «*Legiunea de Jandarmi Năsăud*», Dossier 10/1944-1945

[29] A.N.R.Ms, *Fund cit.*, Dossier 24/1945

[30] *Ibidem.*

[31] A.N.R.O., Fund «*Inspectoratul Judeţean al Jandarmeriei Oradea*», Dossier 2/1944-1945

[32] *Ibidem.*

[33] «*Tribuna Ardealului*», the 15th of December 1944, pp 4

[34] «*Universul*», the 1st of December 1944, pp 3

[35] A.N.I.C., Fund «*Inspectoratul General al Jandarmeriei...*», Dossier 35/1945

[36] «*Tribuna Ardealului*», the 13th of November 1944, pp 17

[37] Ildiko Lipcsey «*Administraţia militară sovietică în Transilvania de Nord (14 noiembrie 1944 – 23 martie 1945)*» in «*Transilvania văzută de publicistica maghiară. Momente din istoria Transilvaniei apărute in revista <<Historia>>*», Ed. Pro-Print, Miercurea Ciuc, 1999, pp 374

[38] A.N.R.O., *Fund. cit.*, Dossier 10/1944-1945

[39] A.N.R.B-ţa, Fund «*Legiunea de Jandarmi Năsăud*», Dossier 2/1944-1945

[40] *Ibidem.*

[41] Corneliu Oprean, Corneliu Nuţ, Ion Pobirci, *op. cit.*, pp 103-104

[42] *Ibidem*, pp 104

[43] *Ibidem.*

[44] A.N.R.B-ta, *Fund cit.*, Dossier 2/1944-1945

[45] *Ibidem*, Dossier 48/1944

[46] *Ibidem.*

[47] *Ibidem.*

[48] Idem, Fund «*Poliţia de Reşedinţă Bistriţa*», Dossier 1/1945

[49] A.N.R.Cluj, Fund «*Inspectoratul de Poliţie Cluj*», Dossier 155/1944

[50] A.N.R.O., *Fund cit.*, Dossier 40/1944

[51] Dumitru Şandru, «*Jandarmeria română. 1944 – 1945*», in « Arhivele Totalitarismului», year II, no.3/1994, pp 229

[52] A.N.I.C., *Fund cit.*, Dossier 3/1944-1945

[53] Dumitru Şandru, «*Regimul cetăţeniei locuitorilor din Nordul Transilvaniei*», in «*Sovietizarea Nord-Vestului României.1944-1945*», Satu-Mare, 1996, pp 65-70

[54] *Ibidem*, pp 71

[55] A.N.R.Cj, *Fund cit.*, Dossier 397/1944-1945

[56] «*Tribuna Ardealului*», the 24th of October 1944, pp 1

[57] A.N.I.C., Fund «*Inspectoratul General al Jandarmeriei...*», Dossier 35/1945, f. 33

[58] Tomas Lonhart, «*Uniunea Populară Maghiară şi chestiunea Transilvaniei (1944-1947)*» in «Transylvanian Review», year IX, no.4, 2000

[59] *Ibidem*, pp 4

[60] Gh. Onişoru, *op. cit.*, pp 184

[61] Tomas Lonhard, *op. cit.*, pp 24

[62] *Ibidem.*

[63] *Ibidem*, pp 25

[64] A.N.I.C., Fund «*Inspectoratul General al Jandarmeriei...*», Dossier 35/1945, f.36

[65] *Ibidem.*

[66] *Ibidem*, Dossier 160/1944-1945

[67] *Ibidem*, Dossier 403/1944-1945

[68] A.N.I.C., *Fund M.A.I.D.A.S.*, Dossier 11/1945

[69] *Idem.*

[70] «*Tribuna Ardealului*», the 25th of November 1944, pp 3

[71] A.N.R.Cluj, Fund «*Inspectoratul de Politie Cluj*», F.397/1944-1946

[72] A.N.I.C., Fund «*Inspectoratul general al Jandarmeriei*», Dossier 35/1945

[73] *Ibidem.*

[74] Vasile Puşcaş, «*Conflicte naţionale şi teritoriale în Europa Central-Răsăriteană şi impunerea dominaţiei sovietice (1944 – 1947)*» in «*Tribuna*»,

new series, IV, no.26, 2-8, July 1992, pp 9

[75] A.N.I.C., *Fund cit.*, Dossier 355/1945

[76] *Ibidem.*

[77] A.N.R.Cluj, Biroul de Cenzură Cluj – Turda, Dossier 9/1944-1945

[78] *Ibidem*, Dossier 160/1944

[79] *Ibidem*, see also A.N.R.B-ţa, Fund «*Prefectura Judeţului Năsăud*», Dossier 120/1944

[80] «*Constituirea comunităţii evreieşti*» in «*Tribuna Ardealului*», the 21st of October 1944, pp 1

[81] Chief Rabbi Dr. Moses Rosen «*Primejdii, încercări, miracole*», ed. Hasefer, Bucharest, 1990, pp 60

[82] Moshe Carmilly – Weinberger «*The help extended by the Romanian Jewish leaders to the Hungarian Jews in the time of the holocaust*» in «*Studia Judaica*», IV, ed. Sincron, Cluj-Napoca, pp 11

[83] *Ibidem.*

[84] «*Memorial. Volume For The Jews of Cluj-Kolozsvar*», edited by Dr. Moshe Carmilly-Weinberger, New – York, 1970, pp 250

[85] *Ibidem*, pp 250-251

[86] A.N.R. Cluj, Fund «*Biroul de Cenzura Cluj-Turda*», Dossier 9/1944-1945

[87] *Ibidem.*

[88] *Ibidem.*

[89] *Ibidem.*

[90] Lowy Daniel «*A teglagyartol a tehervonatig Kolozsvar zsidoo lakossagonak tortenete*», Erdelyi Szepmives Ceh, Kolozsvar, 1998, pp 236

[91] *Ibidem.*

[92] *Ibidem.*

[93] «*Universul*», the 13th of November 1944, pp 3

[94] «*Volt egyszer egy Des. Bethlen. Magyarlapos, Retteg, Nagyilonda es Kornyeke*», vol.III, Tel Aviv, P.OO. B., 202, 1969, pp 593

[95] «*Memorial. Volume...*», pp 252

[96] «Volt egyszer egy...», pp 598

[97] A.N.R.B-ţa, Fund «*Prefectura Judeţului Năsăud*», Dossier 61/1944

[98] A.N.R.Ms, Fund «*Poliţia Judeţului Mureş*», Dossier 35/1944-1945

[99] A.N.R.Cj, *Fund cit.*, Dossier 159/1944

[100] A.N.R.Ms, *Fund cit.*, Dossier 38/1944-1945

[101] A.N.R.B-ţa, Fund «*Poliţia de Reşedinţa Bistriţa*», Dossier 4/1945

[102] A.N.I.C., Fund *M.A.I.D.A.S.*, Dossier 86/1945

[103] A.N.R.Ms, Fund «*Legiunea de Jandarmi Mureş. Secţia Jandarmi Teaca*», Dossier 2/1944-1945

[104] A.N.R.Cj., *Fund cit.*, Dossier 159/1944

[105] Doru Radosav, «*Dombas. O istorie deportata*», ed. Ravensburg, 1994

[106] *Ibidem.*

[107] *Ibidem.*

[108] On the 8th of January 1945, in the village of Sanislău from the district of Sălaj, nowadays in Satu-Mare, there were arrested 414 people, mainly Romanians, that were transported, after being entrained together with the Saxons, to an unknown destination. Cases like this happened also in other localities, Carei, Tăşnad etc. Doru Radosav affirms that, according to another document of May 1945, in January 1945 there have been deported from Sanislău 418 people, from which there were 94 Romanians and 76 Hungarians.

[109] Antonio Faur, «*Măsuri legislative şi economico-administrative de aplicare a Convenţiei de Armistiţiu (septembrie 1944 – mai 1945). Documente*», Fundaţia Culturală «Cele trei Crişuri», Oradea, 1995, pp 4

[110] «*Jurnalul Generalului Constantin Sănătescu – Memorii*», Ed. Humanitas, Bucharest, 1993

[111] A.N.R.O., *Fund cit.*, Dossier 2/1944-1945

[112] *Ibidem.*

[113] A.N.R.B-ţa, Fund «*Prefectura Judeţului Năsăud*», Dossier 48/1944

[114] A.N.R.B-ta, Fund «*Gustav Zikeli...*», pp 76 – 79

[115] A.N.R.O, *Fund cit.*, Dossier 2/1944-1945 and, also, Antonio Faur «*Contribuţii documentare inedite cu privire la raporturile armatei sovietice*

cu populația Bihorului (în lunile septembrie – octombrie 1944)» in «Cetatea Bihariei», 1994, no.3, pp 4-5, no.4, pp 3

[116] *Ibidem.*

[117] A.N.R.Cj., Fund «*Prefectura Județului Cluj*», Dossier 3/1945

[118] *Ibidem*, Dossier 7/1945

[119] Antonio Faur, *op. cit.*, pp 4

[120] A.N.R.B-ța, Fund «*Prefectura Județului Năsăud*», Dossier 39/ 1944

[121] A.N.R.Cj., *Fund cit.*, Dossier 3/1945

[122] *Ibidem.*

[123] A.N.R.B-ța, Fund «*Legiunea de Jandarmi Năsăud*», Dossier 10/1944-1945

[124] *Ibidem.*

[125] Antonio Faur, *op. cit.*

[126] A.N.R.Cluj, *Fund cit.*, Dossier 1/1945

[127] *Ibidem.*

[128] A.N.R.Cluj, Fund «*Inspectoratul de Politie Cluj*», Dossier 155/1944, 397/ 1944-1945, 487/1944-1945

[129] *Ibidem.*

[130] Stephen D. Kertesz, «*Between Russia and West. Hungary and the illusions of Peacemaking 1945 – 1947*», University of Notre Dame Press, London

[131] «*Tribuna Ardealului*», the 10th of December 1944, pp 4

[132] *Ibidem*, the 23rd of December 1944, pp 4

[133] A.N.R.Cj., *Fund cit.*, Dossier 159/1944, 164/1944-1945, 397/1944-1945, 628/ 1944-1945 and A.N.R.B-ta, *Fund cit.*, Dossier 10/1944

[134] *Ibidem.*

[135] *Ibidem.*

[136] Antonio Faur, «*Destinul tragic al românilor basarabeni și bucovineni aflați pe teritoriul Bihorului (1944-1945). Documente*», Presa Universitară Clujeană, Cluj-Napoca, 1998, pp 39

[137] A.N.R., Fund «*Prefectura Județului Mureș*», Dossier 5/1944, f.1

[138] Dumitru Şandru, «*Regimul cetăţeniei locuitorilor din Nordul Transilvaniei*» in «*Sovietizarea Nord-Vestului României 1944-1950*», Ed. Muzeului Sătmărean, Satu-Mare, 1996, pp 65-74

[139] A.N.I.C., Fund «*Inspectoratul General al Jandarmeriei*», Dossier 35/1945

[140] Jacques De Launay, «*Marea prăbuşire, 1944-1945*», Polirom, 1996, pp 1

[141] A.N.I.C., Fund «*Ministerul Afacerilor Interne. Direcţia Administraţiei de Stat*», (M.A.I.D.A.S.), Dossier 22/1944-1945

[142] *Ibidem.*

[143] *Ibidem.*

[144] A.N.R.Ms., *Fund cit.*, Dossier 5/1944

[145] *Ibidem.*

[146] Ion Mureşan, *op. cit.*, pp 266 – 276

[147] Ioan Lăcustă, « *Viaţa românească s-a refugiat la sate*», in «Magazin istoric», year XXIX, no.2, February 1995, pp 26

[148] Ioan Lăcustă, *op. cit.*, pages 25 – 26; also A.N.R.B-ţa, *Fund cit.*, Dossier 59/1944

[149] Ioan Mureşan, *op. cit.*, pp 263

[150] Dănuţ Pop, «*Judeţul Sălaj în timpul administraţiei militare sovietice (noiembrie 1944 – martie 1945). Aspecte ale vieţii economice.*» in «*Sovietizarea Nord-Vestului României...*», pp 105

[151] A.N.I.C., *Fund cit.*, Dossier 21/1944

[152] A.N.R.Ms, Fund «*Prefectura Judeţului Mureş*», Dossier 230/1944

[153] *Ibidem.*

[154] A.N.R.Cluj, Fund «*Biroul de Cenzură Cluj-Turda*», the 20th of November 1944, no. 459

[155] *Ibidem.*

[156] *Idem*, Dossier 9/1944-1945

[157] «*Tribuna Ardealului*», the 12th of December 1944, pp 3

[158] *Idem*, the 16th of January 1945, pp 4

[159] *Idem*, the 18th of January 1945, pp 4

[160] Dănuţ Pop, *op. cit.*, pp 105

[161] *Ibidem*, pp 105

[162] A.N.I.C., Fund «*Inspectoratul General al Jandarmeriei...*», Dossier 26/1944

[163] A.N.R.B-ta, *Fund cit.*, Dossier 122/1944, 253/1944

[164] «*Universul*», the 19th of March 1945, pp 1

[165] *Ibidem.*

[166] «*Tribuna Ardealului*», the 8th of December 1944, pp 4

[167] «*Universul*», the 1st of January 1945, pp 2

[168] *Ibidem.*

[169] «*Universul*», the 15th of November 1944, pp 3

[170] «*Tribuna Ardealului*», the 12th of November 1944

[171] A.N.R.Cj., Fund «*Inspectoratul de Politie Cluj*», Dossier 46/1944-1945; «*Tribuna Ardealului*», the 5th of December 1944, pp 4

[172] Florea Marin «*Iuliu Haţieganu. Monografie*», Ed. Universităţii de Medicină şi Farmacie «Iuliu Haţieganu», Cluj-Napoca, 1999, pp 145

[173] *Ibidem*, pp 146

[174] Idem, «*Furtuni în centrul medical clujean*», Ed. Universităţii de Medicină şi Farmacie «Iuliu Haţieganu», Cluj-Napoca, 1998, pp 73

[175] *Ibidem.*

[176] Idem, «*Iuliu Haţieganu. Monografie*», pp 146

[177] *Ibidem*, pp 148

[178] «*Tribuna Ardealului*», the 12th of December 1944 and no. 1194, the 19th of December 1944

[179] Dănuţ Pop, *op. cit.*, pp 106

[180] A.N.R.B-ţa, *Fund cit.*, Dossier 23/1944

[181] *Ibidem.*

[182] *Ibidem.*

[183] *Ibidem.*

[184] Ioan Mureşan, *op. cit.*, pp 266

[185] A.N.R.Ms, *Fund cit.*, Dossier 1/1944

[186] *Ibidem*, Dossier 305/1944

[187] A.N.R.Cluj, Fund «*Biroul de Cenzură Cluj – Turda*», Dossier 9/1944-1945

[188] «*Tribuna Ardealului*», the 3rd of December 1944, pp 2

[189] *Ibidem*, the 30th of November 1944, pp 4

[190] *Ibidem.*

[191] *Idem*, the 3rd of December 1944, pp 3

[192] *Ibidem.*

[193] A.N.R.Cluj, *Fund cit.*, Dossier 9/1944-1945

[194] «*Tribuna Ardealului*», the 23rd of January 1945, pp 3

[195] A.N.R.Cluj, *Fund cit.*, Dossier 9/1944-1945

[196] «*Tribuna Ardealului*», the 24th of November 1944, pp 4 and no. 1186-1187, the 14th -15th of December 1944, pp 2

[197] *Idem*, the 29th of November 1944, pp 44

[198] *Idem*, the 14th of December 1944, pp 2

[199] *Ibidem.*

[200] *Idem*, the 2nd of December 1944, pp 4

[201] *Ibidem.*

[202] *Idem*, the 21st of December 1944, pp 2

[203] Liviu Ţîrău «*Dezvoltarea structurilor de putere ale Partidului Comunist Român în judeţul Cluj 1945 – 1946*», in «*Anuarul Istitutului de Istorie*», Cluj, XXX/1993, pp 277-278

[204] *Ibidem*, pp 278

[205] A.N.R.Cluj, *Fund cit.*, Dossier 403/1944 – 1945

[206] *Ibidem.*

[207] A.N.R.Cluj, *Fund cit.*, Dossier 9/1944-1945

[208] «*România. Viaţa politică în documente*», doc. no. 6

[209] *Ibidem.*

[210] Vasile Vesa, Marcela Sălăgean «*From Soviet administration in Transylvania to nationalist frictions between Romanian and Hungarian communists*» in «*Romanian and British historians on the contemporary history of Romania*», ed. by George Cipăianu and Virgiliu Ţîrău, Cluj University Press, 2000, pp 141

[211] *Ibidem*, pp 140

[212] A.N.R.Cj., *Fund cit.*, Dossiers 159/1944, 164/1944, 170/1944-1945, 397/1944-1945, 628/1944-1946, 635/1944-1946, 751/1944-1946

[213] *Ibidem*, Dossiers 155/1944, 412/1944-1945, 478/1944-1946, 635/1944-1946, 754/1944-1946

[214] *Ibidem.*

[215] «*Tribuna Ardealului*», the 19th of November 1944, pp 1

[216] *Idem*, the 21st of November 1944, page 3; «*Universul*», the 26th of November 1944, pp 3

[217] *Ibidem.*

[218] *Ibidem.*

[219] *Ibidem*, Dossier 478/1944-1946

[220] *Ibidem*, Dossier 751/1944-1946

[221] *Ibidem.*

[222] Vlad Georgescu, *op. cit.*, pp 248-253

[223] Ilie Chercheş, «*Situaţia naţională şi viaţa politică a Maramureşului...*», pp 286

[224] *Ibidem.*

[225] A.N.I.C., Fund «*Inspectoratul General al Jandarmeriei*», Dossier 28/1944

[226] *Ibidem.*

[227] Ilie Chercheş, *op. cit.*, pp 287

[228] *Ibidem.*

[229] A.N.I.C., Rola 6636, M. 006 S.U.A., 1080 c, f. 8

[230] *Ibidem.*

[231] *Ibidem.*

[232] Ilie Chercheş, *op. cit.*, pp 290

[233] Florin Muller, «*Tentative de rapt teritorial şi de sovietizare a regiunii Maramureş în anii 1944 – 1945*» in «*Revista istorică*», vol.IV, no. 7-8, July – August 1993, pp 699

[234] A.N.I.C., Rola 636...

[235] Florin Muller, *op. cit.*, pp 701

[236] Ilie Chercheş, *op. cit.*, pp 291

[237] *Ibidem.*

[238] Florin Muller, *op. cit.*, pp 701-702

[239] A.N.I.C., Rola 636...

[240] A.N.I.C., Fund «*Inspectoratul General al Jandarmeriei...*», Dossier 28/ 1944

[241] Florin Muller, *op. cit.*, pp 703-704

[242] A.N.R.Cluj, Fund «*Inspectoratul de Politie Cluj*», Dossier 397/1944-1945

CHAPTER FIVE

THE REESTABLISHMENT OF THE ROMANIAN ADMINISTRATION IN NORTHERN TRANSYLVANIA

The conclusion of the Armistice Convention between the United Nations and Hungary has represented an important moment for northern Transylvania. Signed in the final part of January 1945, the Convention stipulated in its second article that «Hungary accepts and obliges itself to evacuate all the Hungarian troups and official authorities from the territories of Czechoslovakia, Yugoslavia and Romania inside the Hungarian borders existing on the 31st of December 1937 and it pledges itself to render void all the legislative and administrative stipulations referring to the annexation or the joining of these territories»[1], that was in fact the annulment of the Vienna Award, event transmitted by the A.F.I. agency on the 25th of January.

Immediately after that day, the frequency of the appeals addressed to the Soviet Union by the National Peasant and liberal leaders for the retrocession of northern Transylvania to the romanian state has intensified. The liberals have published, in their newspaper «Viitorul», a programme for the reconstruction of the northern Transylvanian districts.[2] Even the governing programme of the National Democratic Front, published on the 29th of January 1945, included dispositions concerning the northern Transylvania's return to the administrative and political structures of the Romanian state and also dispositions concerning the prevention and the stopping of the interethnic incidents.[3] Taking a stand against the publishing of the F.N.D.'s programme, the liberals have accused, at the beginning of February 1945 by an official statement, those political formations that made use of the question of northern Transylvania and of the repatriation of the Romanian prisoners as «instruments for Party propaganda»[4].

The statute of northern Transylvania has not been subjected to any change until the installation of the government of dr. Petru Groza, although there were heard rumours and projects regarding its future or the entire Transylvania's future, after the 12th of November 1944, both in Romania and Hungary and in Western Europe. Thus, a few days after the removal of the Romanian civil servants from the civil and military institutions of northern Transylvania, a group of personalities representing the Reformed Church from the United States tried to offer new arguments (that reached the Peace Conference's table) in favour of the idea of an independent Transylvania, considering that «it represents the most eastern part of the Western world, while Romania (the Old Kingdom) is, on the contrary, the most western part of the Orient»[5].

Back in the country, most of the rumours, which many times did nothing but express the frustrated aspirations of the vanquished, have going about mainly in the great cities, especially in Cluj, city that was considered to be the spiritual capital of the Transylvanian Hungarians.

Thus, the reports of the Intelligence Service of the period from December 1944 to March 1945 show an interest directed above all on northern Transylvania. Here we have a few suggestive examples:

December the 1st, 1944, note no.483

«...The Soviet Union tries to create an independent republic in northern Transylvania. This republic, with its democratic government, would decree the joining to the Soviet Union. By doing this, it is tried to open a large way towards the centre of Europe. The Soviet Union sees that, because of the spirit of the Romanian people, it will not be able to bring Romania directly in the situation of the Baltic states. In this manner, a factual state would be created at the Peace Conference and, on the other hand, it would even indirectly force Romania to tie its fate to the Soviet union's will. The discussions related to this matter are very vehement within the Romanian circles, which accuse the government of weakness and even of betraying the Romanian people's interest»[6].

December the 30th, 1944, note no. 502

«By the order of the Hungarian government, recently established in Debrecen, the merchants of Cluj have refused, beginning with yesterday, the 29th of December 1944, to accept Romanian lei (the Romanian currency), as payment. That happened as a result of the defeat of Budapest. Soon, a statement of this government will be made,according to which Hungary would be decreed as Republic affiliated to the Soviet Union, as a national state, having in the interim under its administration all the territories from 1940, conformable to the convention that it has from 1942. Northern and southern Transylvania would be declared republic, through a change of government, with some cultural autonomy, within the Hungarian state. These changes in Hungary[7] will also have significant consequences upon our situation, in the Balkans».

December the 31st, 1944, note no. 503

«As for the recent developments from Hungary and the leaving of a delegation of the government from Debrecen in order to conclude an armistice between the Soviet Union and Hungary, the rumours that come in from beyond the Feleac are more and more allarming... The Hungarian delegation that left right now to Moscow does not have the mission to conclude an armistice with Russia, because this armistice has already been concluded in 1942, but to conclude the majority of the Hungarians requirements, aproved by Russia in the secret treaty of 1942, the winter and the spring of 1943. In accordance with that treaty, as soon as the Soviet Union forces the Carpathians gorges, Hungary would attack the rear of the German – Romanian front, opening thus the way to Vienna and Berlin. However, it is known that this plan has been baffled by the coup d'etat of the 23st of August 1944 and the coup of Sallasi. According to this meaning, Hungary, on one side, and the entire Transylvania – both the northern and the southern -, on the other side, would be independent republics, under the sovereignty of the U.S.S.R., just like the Baltic countries. The southern Transylvania's administration would be made in two languages, in Hungarian and in Romanian. In addition to these, Oltenia would be annexed to Hungary, up to north of Craiova, also Croatia and eastern Slavonia and Ruscinsco. A particular desideratum is represented by the free harbour by the Black Sea, in the radius of Constanţa, the railway line Constanţa – Nehoiaş – Arad – Budapest... Here it is the main cause for the evacuation of northern Transylvania by the Romanian army and administration. It is to be handed over to the administration of the government from Debrecen, even before the conclusion of the Soviet – Hungarian armistice treaty. The very occupation of southern Transylvania is just a question of time...»[8]

All this information makes evident the concern regarding the double dealing game of the Soviet Union, which was decided to subordinate, by any means, these territories, by maintaining a state of uncertainty with regard to their future. At the same time, these rumours have found an increasingly favourable ground in the Romanian public opinion, the pessimism and the depression becoming more and more pronounced.

As for Romania, the Soviets have known how to exploit to a maximum the Romanian – Hungarian conflicts, succeeding in transforming the nationalists in conjectural communists, supporters of their cause. They have maintained the illusion of the possibility of some other solutions for northern Transylvania, other than its return to Romania, as they have massively infiltrated in the leftist political and trade unionist organizations, supported by the Soviets. The rumours of those times have grasped, in fact, the great unrest of the population of northern Transylvania, its fears and its hopes. Facts as the presence of the Soviet troops, the abuses committed by the soldiers, the economic uncertainty, the participation to the military operations from beyond the country's borders etc. have had a significant social impact.

After the removal of the Rădescu's government and the success of the Soviet pressures on King Mihai I, who was forced to entrust the mission of forming a new government to Petru Groza, the Romanian communists have found the right moment to make a political capital out of a problem that, in fact, had already been decided by the Soviets long ago.

The moment they got the power, the Petru Groza government had the task to put into practice the decisions taken at the F.N.D.'s meeting. Thus, the first step was the reinstatement of northern Transylvania within Romania. In this direction were made the statements of Petru Groza with regard to the Transylvanian question. Short after its investment as Prime Minister, he has declared that a F.N.D. government may obtain the repatriation of tens of thousands of prisoners and the leave to enter in northern Transylvania with pride. On its government's programme, Groza has stated that he had the hope that the question of Transylvania will be settled.[9]

On the 8th of March 1945, by a letter addressed to Stalin, the President of the Council of Ministers and to the Minister of Foreign Affairs, it was requested the establishment of the Romanian administration in northern Transylvania, the consent of the generalissim Stalin and of the Soviet government being obtained no later than the following day. That recognition was made, thus, not by virtue of the Romanian right of sovereignty over this territory, but as a reward given to the nation for the accepting of a «democratic» (pro-communist) government by the King. The fact that the whole action was, actually, just a means for blackmail results also from the findings that the same stipulations of the Armistice Convention that were invoked by the Soviets in November 1944 for the removal of the Romanian administration from northern Transylvania were mentioned by Stalin in the letter addressed to Petru Groza on the 9th of March 1945, though this time for justifying the reinstatement of this administration.[10] That is, in order to create among the people a favourable environment to the government they had imposed at the head of Romania, the Soviet occupation authorities agreed on the 9th of March on the reinstatement of the Romanian administration in northern Transylvania.

The last episode of the life of the Romanian Commissariate for the administration of liberated Transylvania has been consumed in that period. The setting up of the Groza government has determined the resignation of the High Commissary Ionel Pop, fact that actually meant the ceasing of this institution's activity.[11]

Of course, the «friendly» gesture of the Soviet Union and the great achievement of the Groza government have not remained without echoes. On the 9th of March also, the Reuter Agency has transmitted the news that mentioned that during the previous governments of generals Sănătescu and Rădescu, the promise to retrocede Transylvania has not been fulfilled and that the Soviet government was not at all anxious about the nonfulfilment of that condition. It was thus obvious that Groza was «persona grata» for the Russians.[12]

On the 11th of March, London radio station, the programme in Romanian, referring on the act of the 9th of March, noticed the following: «is is an interesting fact that this thing happens six months after the conclusion of the armistice that stipulates the annulment of the Vienna Award»[13] . The answer to that delay has been given by Vishinsky, onthe 12th of March, when he stated that Transylvania has been liberated by the Red Army and the Soviet government was ready at that time to introduce the Romanian administration in Transylvania. However, the conditions for achieving that decision were not auspicious in Kremlin's opinion.[14]

After the statement made on radio by the Chairman of the Council of Ministers, regarding the return of the Romanian administration in northern Transylvania, the reaction of the region's population has been based on their own interests. From the documents existent in the archives, the following conclusions can be drawn with regard to the state of mind of the Romanians and of the Hungarians. The Romanians were pretty skeptical. Very few believed that the U.S.S.R. would maintain further on the present situation, that it would make promises with a set date, but it would allways find reasons for delay, respectively for unfulfilment.[15] The Hungarians were astounded. They did not want the Romanian authorities to enter in northern Transylvania. They accused them of being reactionary, nazi, Hitlerite, fascist etc. and said that they do not belong in the region.[16]

The analysis of the regime set up in northern Transylvania in November 1944, from a social, economic and political point of view, leads us to the conclusion that, although it has impeded the scaling of the interethnic tensions, it did not succeed to operate upon their causes, which will remain a target for the Romanian government. Also, the moment the Romanian administration has reinstated, the northern Transylvanian districts were to know, the same with the whole country, a new evolution, as a result of which they have entered under the rule of the communist regime.

Actually, by taking northern Transylvania out of the authority of the Romanian administration, dynamizing discreetly the Romanian – Hungarian animosity, deluding the Hungarians, the fate of which was already decided, and, at the same time, blackmailing the Romanians,

Stalin has got the installation of a communist government in Bucharest, the Bessarabian and the Bukovinean territories and the participation of the Romanian troops in the western war, and also a submissive attitude and a lack of combativity on the part of Budapest.

The Soviets were the ones to decide, in fact, as early as in 1944, the future of northern Transylvania, deliberately baffling all the British – American attempts to provide some other solution, more convenient to Hungary, to this problem. Responding to the British – American protests, that accused Stalin of giving northern Transylvania to Romania without taking their advice, general Susaikov has serenely declared that «Transylvania has not been returned to Romania, all that happened was that the Romanian administration has been permitted to enter in northern Transylvania in order to administrate it, in anticipation of the Peace Conference's decision»[17].

All this time, the reinstatement of the Romanian administration in northern Transylvania, already considered to be a final solution, has been celebrated with great enthusiasm and joy, in public meetings where the representatives of the Groza government and of the communist party have known how to put themselves forward.

On the 13th of March, in Cluj have taken place festivities occasioned by this event, to which there have participated King Mihai, members of the government, A. Vishinsky, the patriarch Nicodim etc. After the festivities, a solemn meeting of the Council of Ministers has taken place, to which has participated, also, Vishinsky.[18] The moment they got the Soviet Union's assent, the Romanian government has passed to the approval of some legislative measures, necessary to the reinstatement of the Romanian administration in northern Transylvania. Thus, on the 30th of March 1945, a conference of the prefects from northern Transylvania has taken place and, on that occasion, the Prime Minister Petru Groza has asked them to eliminate the chauvinism, affirming that a better understanding between the Romanians and the Hungarians would hasten the process of integrating Transylvania within the Romanian state.[19] In fact, Groza knew that such a policy of supporting the Hungarian minority made necessary additional efforts to gain the Romanians' sympathy. In this way, in order to provide for themselves a real support in the Romanian society, through declarations and measures meant to rectify some wrongs, the communists have tried to create a different image than the one that was attributed to them. Using the ascendency obtained by the success of the 9th of March 1945, well exploited by the propaganda, the communists have contended that the good relations of the Romanians with the coinhabiting nationalities were strictly needed for maintaining the territorial status quo, in anticipation of the Peace Conference from Paris. In these circumstances, a whole series of measures have been applied in favour of the minorities, in the spheres of the culture, religious life, law etc.[20] and even though it did not succeed to eliminate the interethnic tensions, the Groza government's policy has succeeded at least to attenuate them. The efforts have been lasting a long time and the conditions, that left the authorities very little liberty of movement, have been extremely difficult.

In the framework of the same meeting from the end of March 1945, Lucreţiu Pătrăşcanu considered that it was needed a real and fair purification in order to create a new administration, which would be able to change the former structure.[21] According to the law no. 260 of the 3rd of April 1945, the Romanian legislation has extended over the entire territory of northern Transylvania. As for the appointed staff, at the level of the districts there have been maintained the same persons, in the main. Anyway, if at the superior level the situation has remained almost unchanged, the other levels have undergone through a series of changes, caused mainly by the transferring of functionaries from other Romanian districts. For example, on the 4th of April 1945, the government has sent to the prefect's office of the district of Satu-Mare civil servants from Hunedoara, Olt, Sibiu, Muscel, Severin, Mehedinţi, Dâmboviţa and Arad.[22]

NOTES:

[1] «*23 August 1944. Documente...*», doc. nr. 1108

[2] «*Tribuna Ardealului*», the 24th of January 1945, pp 4

[3] *Ibidem*, the 29th of January 1945; also, «*23 August 1944. Documente...*», doc. no. 1123

[4] *Ibidem*, vol.IV, doc. no. 1209

[5] A.N.I.C., Rola 630771c M006, S.U.A.

[6] A.N.R.Cluj, Fund «*Biroul de Cenzură Cluj-Turda*», Dossier 9/1944-1945

[7] *Ibidem.*

[8] *Ibidem.*

[9] «*23 August. Documente*», vol.IV, doc. no. 1231

[10] «*România. Viața politică în documente.1945*», pp 197-198

[11] Ion Silviu Nistor, *op. cit.*, pp 497-498

[12] «*23 August 1944. Documente*», no. 1251

[13] *Ibidem*, doc. no.1255

[14] *Ibidem.*

[15] A.N.R.Cj., Fund «*Biroul de Cenzură Cluj – Turda*», Dossier 9/1944-1945

[16] *Ibidem.*

[17] Nicoleta Franck «*O înfrângere în victorie*», Ed. Humanitas, Bucharest, 1992

[18] «*România. Viața politică în documente*», doc. no. 1290

[19] «*23 August 1944. Documente*», doc. no. 1290; Vasile Vesa, Marcela Sălăgean, op. cit., pp 141

[20] *Ibidem.*

[21] «*23 August. Documente*», Doc. no. 1291

[22] Claudiu Porumbăceanu, *op. cit.*

CONCLUSION

The decision to establish an allied (Soviet) military administration in northern Transylvania has been taken, thus, long before November 1944; the same can be said also about the Moscow's decision to use this territory as a means for blackmail that was to be exercised simultaneously on the governments from Budapest and Bucharest. In such conditions, the attempt to explain the taking of that decision by the political conjuncture of November 1944 would do nothing but create confusion. On the contrary, much more useful would be the adequate explanation of the reasons that made the Soviets allow for a short while, in the autumn of 1944, the return of the Romanian administration in few of the liberated Transylvanian districts.

This option has been based, in essence, upon a series of tactical grounds. It had, in the first place, the role of providing the Moscow's agents infiltrated within the structures of decision from Bucharest the period of time needed to consolidate their positions. As a matter of fact, it could be noticed that it was precisely the government crisis from the beginning of November that represented, in fact, the sign of the Communist Party's open entry in the struggle for power, fact that had as an immediate consequence the removal of the Romanian administration from northern Transylvania. From that moment on, the Soviets had no reasons to show tolerance towards any non-communist government from Bucharest.

Also, the setting up of some rudiments of Romanian administration has contributed to the support of the spirits of the Romanian troops that carried on military operations in the area. These troups would have hardly understood and accepted, undoubtedly, the keeping of an administration with Hungarian functionaries in Romanian territories liberated as a result of bloody battles carried against the same Hungarians. In the same circumstances, it is possible that the Soviets had speculated from the very beginning on the occurence of some interethnic incidents, in the mean time, which would have given them an excellent justification to assume the role of champions of the interethnic stability and of arbitrators of the Romanian – Hungarian relations.

Not in the last place, the tolerance showed by the Soviets towards the provisional establishment of the Romanian administrative structures can also be seen as an implicit recognition (a provisional one, it's true) of the Bucharest's merits in the act of the 23rd of August 1944 and, also, as a very cautious Moscow's declaration of intention toward the future of northern Transylvania. However, the real meaning of this decision was not different from the warning represented by the other decision to remove the Romanian administration, at the beginning of November: there were two messages clearly addressed to Romania's leaders, that had to understand that, as for northern Transylvania, Moscow had already gained by force the right to have the last word.

As it has been seen from the very beginning of the great world wide conflagration, Romania – the same with the other small states from Central and Eastern Europe trapped in the great turmoil – was actually far from being its real own master, as it was reduced to the role of a pawn, the importance of which was the more difficult to define as the game had this time world wide proportions. Romania could do but to influence, as much as possible, the decisions of the Great Powers, fructifying, with maximum of efficiency and at the right time, the few trumps it had in hand. In this way, the historical decision taken by King Mihai I and the leaders of the main democratical parties on the 23rd of August 1944 has had an enormous importance – by the fact that it has been accomplished long before the already prepared similar move on the part of Hungary – as it was able to eliminate many of the uncertainties that hung over the post war fate of Transylvania.

The developments of the following months, however, have brought out the huge discrepancy existing between the aspirations of the democratical political forces from Romania and the cruel geopolitical reality. The tense anxiety that has been the characteristic, all that time, of the life of the northern Transylvanian inhabitants has made but to reflect the difficulties of their adjustment to the new historical reality. Trapped in the tangled thicket of the rumours and disinformation emanated from the political centers that were interested in the faith of that territory (Bucharest, Budapest, Moscow), this region's inhabitants, whether they were Romanians, Hungarians, Germans, Jews or Ukraineans, have lived moments of serious ordeal, that have added to the inherent difficulties caused by the war, have shaped plans, have cherished hopes and, in many cases, have suffered bitter disappointments. The Moscow's implacable will has made that, in the end, none of them would enjoy the satisfaction of a complete success. That thing has remained, for a long period of time, an exclusive privilege of the representatives of the Stalinist communism.

GENERAL BIBLIOGRAPY

I – SOURCES

A – Archive sources

Arhivele Naţionale Istorice Centrale – A.N.I.C.
(The Central Historical National Archives):
Inspectoratul General al Jandarmeriei
Ministerul Afacerilor Interne.
Direcţia Administraţiei de Stat
Ministerul Afacerilor Interne- Diverse
Preşedenţia Consiliului de Miniştri
Arhivele Ministerului Afacerilor Externe
(The Archive of the Ministry of Foreign Affairs),
Fond 71 Transilvania
Arhivele Naţionale Române Cluj-Napoca – A.N.R.Cj
(The Romanian National Archive of Cluj-Napoca):
Inspectoratul de Poliţie Cluj
Inspectoratul de Jandarmi Cluj
Prefectura Judeţului Cluj
Biroul Armistiţiu
Biroul de Cenzură Cluj – Turda
Comitetul Judeţean al Partidului Comunist Român
Chestura Poliţiei Cluj
Inspectoratul General Administrativ Cluj
Arhivele Naţionale Române Bistriţa – A.N.R.B-ţa
(The Romanian National Archive of Bistriţa):
Legiunea de Jandarmi a Judeţului Năsăud
Poliţia de Reşedinţa Bistriţa
Prefectura Judeţului Năsăud
«Gustav Zikeli»
Arhivele Naţionale Române Tg-Mureş – A.N.R.Tg-Ms
(The Romanian National Archive of Târgu-Mureş):
Legiunea de Jandarmi Mureş
Prefectura Judeţului Mureş
Arhivele Naţionale Române Oradea – A.N.R.O.
(The Romanian National Archive of Oradea):
Inspectoratul de Jandarmi Oradea

B – The Press

Tribuna Ardealului
Universul
Dreptatea
Scânteia
Ardealul
Tribuna Ardealului, new series

C – Collections of documents

23 August 1944. Documente 1944-1945, Ed. Ştiinţifică şi Enciclopedică, Bucharest, 1985

Faur Antonio, *Destinul tragic al românilor basarabeni şi bucovineni aflaţi pe teritoriul Bihorului (1944-1945). Documente*, Presa Universitară Clujeană, Cluj-Napoca, 1998

Pop Ştefan I, *O pagină de istorie. Viaţa judeţului Năsăud de la 13 octombrie 1944 la 13 martie 1945*, Tipografia Minerva Bistriţa, 1947

România în anii celui de-al doilea război mondial, Ed. Militară, Bucharest, 1989

România, marele sacrificat al celui de-al doilea război mondial. Documente, ed. by Marin Radu Mocanu, vol.I, Bucharest, 1994

România, viaţa politică în documente, 1945, ed. by Ioan Scurtu, Bucharest, 1994

Romanian Military Structures Involved in the Enforcement of the Armistice Agreement and the Treaty of Peace Finding Aid, vol.I, 1944-1948, ed. Militară, Bucharest, 1999

Zamfirescu Dragoş, *Documente referitoare la prezenţa armatei sovietice pe teritoriul României*, Bucharest, 1998

D – Memoirs

Motru Rădulescu Constantin, *Revizuiri şi adăugiri*, 1944-1945, vol.II-III, ed. Floarea Darurilor, Bucharest, 1996

Sănătescu Constantin, *Jurnal*, ed. Humanitas, Bucharest, 1993

Schuyler C.V.R., *Misiune dificilă. Jurnal (28 ianuarie 1945 – 20 septembrie 1946)*, ed. Enciclopedică, Bucharest, 1997

Ţepelea Gabriel, *Amintiri şi evocări*, ed. Fundaţiei Culturale Române, Bucharest, 1994

Ţepelea Gabriel, *Însemnări de taină*, ed. Fundaţiei Culturale Române, Bucharest, 1997

Ţepelea Gabriel, *Secvenţe din purgatoriu*, ed. Fundaţiei Culturale Române, Bucharest, 1999

II – GENERAL AND SPECIAL STUDIES

Alexandrescu Ion, *Reinstalarea autorităţilor civile româneşti în teritoriul cedat Ungariei în urma «Arbitrajului» de la Viena din 30 August 1940*, in *Anuarul Institutului pentru studii politice de apărare şi istorie militară*, Bucharest, 1996

Antohe Ion, *Răstigniri în România după Yalta*, ed. Albatros, Bucharest, 1995

Arhivele Totalitarismului, Institutul Naţional pentru Studiul Totalitarismului

Baciu Nicolae, *Agonia României, 1944-1948. Dosare secrete acuză*, ed. Dacia, Cluj-Napoca, 1990

Baciu Nicolae, *Yalta şi crucificarea României*, Ed. Europa, Bucharest, 1996

Barker Elisabeth, *British Policy in South-East Europe in the Second World War*, London, 1976

Baross Gabor, *Hungary and Hitler*, Los Angeles, University of Southern California, 1964

Bodea Gheorghe I., *Încercări de anexare forțată a Maramureșului din stânga Tisei la Ucraina sovietică, octombrie 1944 – mai 1945*, in *Maramureș, vatră de istorie milenară*, no. 4, Cluj-Napoca, 1998

Buzatu Gheorghe, *România cu și fără Antonescu. Documente, studii, relatări și comentarii*, Ed. Moldova, Iași, 1998

Carmilly Weinberger Moshe, *The help extended by the Romanian-Jewish leaders to the Hungarian Jews in the time of the Holocaust* in *Studia Judaica*, IV, 1995

Chercheș Ilie, *Situația națională și viața politică a Maramureșului (octombrie 1944 – ianuarie 1945)* in *Maramureș – vatră de istorie milenară*, Ed. Dragoș-Vodă, Cluj-Napoca, 1997

Chiper Ioan, *Conjunctura semnării armistițiului de la Moscova*, in *Revista istorică*, Bucharest, 1998

Ciachir Nicolae, *Marile Puteri și România, 1856 – 1947*, Ed. Albatros, Bucharest, 1996

Constantiniu Florin, Duțu Alexandru, Retegan Mihai, *România în război 1941 – 1945*, Ed. Militară, Bucharest, 1995

Constantiniu Florin, *De la războiul fierbinte la războiul rece*, Ed. Corint, Bucharest, 1998

Constantiniu Florin, *O istorie sinceră a poporului român*, Ed. Univers Enciclopedic, Bucharest, 1997

Csatari Daniel, *Dans le tournament. Les Relations Hungaro – Roumains de 1940 – 1945*, Budapest, 1974

Dobrinescu Florin Valeriu, *O negare a principiilor de drept internaţional – Problema basarabenilor şi a bucovinenilor în Comisia Aliată de Control (1944 – 1945)*, in *Anuar Fundaţia Academia «Petre Andrei»*, no. 4, 1996

Dobrinescu Florin Valeriu, *România şi Ungaria de la Trianon la Paris (1920 – 1947). Bătălia diplomatică pentru Ardeal*, Ed. Viitorul Românesc, 1996

Dobrinescu Florin Valeriu, *România şi organizarea postbelică a lumii (1945 – 1947)*, Ed. Academiei Republicii Socialiste România, Bucharest, 1988

Dobrinescu Florin Valeriu, *Comisia Aliată de Control (Sovietică) şi interpretarea articolului 19 din Convenţia de Armistiţiu (12 septembrie 1944 – 6 martie 1945)* in *Sovietizarea Nord-Vestului României, 1944-1945*, Satu-Mare, 1996

Deletant Dennis, *Studies in Romanian History*, Ed. Enciclopedică, Bucharest, 1991

Duţu Alexandru, *Anularea Dictatului de la Viena – cauza naţiunii române*, in *Acta Musei Napocensis*, Muzeul de istorie Cluj-Napoca, no. 2, 1995

Faur Antonio, *Măsuri legislative şi economico-administrative de aplicare a Convenţiei de Armistiţiu (septembrie 1944 – mai 1945). Documente*, Ed. Fundaţiei Culturale «Cele trei Crişuri», 1995

Faur Antonio, *Contribuţii documentare la cunoaşterea activităţii delegatului Comisiei Române pentru Aplicarea Armistiţiului*, in «Crisia», XXVI – XXVII, Oradea, 1997

Florea Marin, *Furtuni în centrul medical clujean*, Ed. Universităţii de Medicină şi Farmacie «Iuliu Haţieganu», Cluj-Napoca, 1998

Florea Marin, *Iuliu Haţieganu. Monografie*, Ed. Universităţii de Medicină şi Farmacie «Iuliu Haţieganu», Cluj-Napoca, 1999

Frunză Victor, *Istoria stalinismului în România*, Ed. Humanitas, Bucharest, 1990

Fulop Mihaly, *L'occupation sovietique en Europe central et orientale*, in *Relation Internationales*, 79, 1994

Gardner Lloyd C., *Sferele de influenţă. Împărţirea Europei între marile puteri, de la Munchen la Yalta*, Ed. Elit, 1993

Giurescu Dinu C., *Guvernarea Nicolae Rădescu*, Ed. All, Bucharest, 1996

Hitchins Keith, *România 1866 – 1947*, Ed. Humanitas, Bucharest, 1994

Hlihor Constantin, Ioan Scurtu, *The Red Army in Romania*, Center for Romanian Studies, Iaşi, Oxford, Portland, 2000

Hlihor Constantin, *Armata Roşie în România. Adversar, aliat, ocupant, 1944 – 1948*, vol.I, Academia de Înalte Studii Militare, Bucharest, 1996

Hlihor Constantin, *Ocuparea României de către Armata Roşie. Premise, etape, consecinţe*, in *Revista Istorică*, Bucharest, 1994

Kiriţescu Constantin I., *România în al doilea război mondial*, Vol.I-II, Ed. Univers Enciclopedic, Bucharest, 1995

Launay Jacques, *Marea prăbuşire, 1944-1945*, Ed. Polirom, Iaşi, 1996

Lăcustă Ioan, *12 februarie 1945. Transilvania de Nord, Viaţa românească s-a refugiat la sate*, in *Magazin Istoric*, no. 11, 1997

Lăcustă Ioan, *Cluj, noiembrie 1944 – martie 1945. Uniunea Democrată Română face opoziţie comuniştilor*, in *Magazin Istoric*, no. 12, 1995

Lonhart Tomas, *Uniunea Populară Maghiară şi chestiunea*

Transilvaniei (1944

- 1947) in Transylvanian Review, 4, 2000

Lowy Daniel, *A teglagyartol a tehervonatig Kolozsvar zsido lakossagonak tortenete*, A Kolozsvar Sajtot Schvarcz Rekatallozta, Erdelyi Szepmives Ceh, Kolozsvar, 1998

Max M. Stanley, *The United States, Great Britain and the sovietization of Hungary, 1945 – 1948*, East European Monographs, Boulder, Columbia Univesity Press, 1985

Memorial. Volume for the Jews of Cluj-Kolozsvar, Edited by Dr. Moshe Carmilly-Weinberger, New-York, 1970

Mendev Roy, *Despre Stalin şi stalinism. Consemnări istorice*, Ed. Humanitas, Bucharest, 1991

Muller Florin, *Tentative de rapt teritorial şi de sovietizare a regiunii Maramureş în anii 1944-1945*, in *Revista Istorică*, IV, 1993

Mureşan Ioan, *Situaţia social-politică şi economică din judeţul Năsăud în timpul administraţiei militare sovietice (13 octombrie 1944 – 12 aprilie 1945)* in *Revista Bistriţei*, VII, Muzeul Judeţean Bistriţa-Năsăud, Iaşi-Rădăuţi, Casa Editorială şi de Presă Glasul Bucovinei, 1993

Naimark Norman, Leonid Gibianskii, *The establishment of Communist regimes in Eastern Europe, 1944-1949*, Westview Press, Colorado, United States of America, 1997

Negrea Camil, *Le probleme du retablissment de la Legislation Roumaine en Transylvanie du Nord*, Centrul de studii şi cercetări privitoare la Transilvania, Sibiu, 1945

Nistor Ioan Silviu, *Constituirea şi activitatea Comisariatului pentru administrarea Transilvaniei eliberate (octombrie 1944 – martie 1945)* in *Anuarul Institutului de Istorie şi Arheologie*, Ed. Academiei, Cluj-Napoca, 1983-1984

Nistor Ioan Silviu, *Transilvania de Nord de la administrația militară ungară la administrația militară rusă*, in *Maramureș, vatră de istorie milenară*, no. 1, 1996

Nouzille Jean, *Transylvania an area of contacts and conflicts*, Ed. Enciclopedică, Bucharest, 1996

Onișoru Gheorghe, *România în anii 1944-1948. Transformări economice și realități sociale*, Fundația Academia Civică, Bucharest, 1999

Onișoru Gheorghe, *Statutul nord-vestului Transilvaniei de la 23 august 1944 la 10 februarie 1947*, in Acta Musei Porolissensis, Muzeul de istorie și artă Zalău, 1995

Onofrei Adrian, *Factori de influență politică în activitatea prefecturii județului Năsăud (1944-1947)*, în *Revista Bistriței*, 1999

Oprean Cornel, Corneliu Nuț, Ion Pobirici, *Jandarmeria ardeleană, tradiție și contemporaneitate*, Ed. Dacia, Cluj-Napoca, 1999

Pokivailova Tatiana, *Transilvania pe masa Comisiei Litvinov*, in *Magazin Istoric*, no. 1, 1998

Pop Dănuț, *Județul Sălaj în timpul administrației militare sovietice (noiembrie 1944 – martie 1945). Aspecte ale vieții economice*, in *Sovietizarea Nord-Vestului României*, Satu-Mare, 1996

Porter Ivor, *Operațiunea «Autonomous» în România în vreme de război*, Ed. Humanitas, Bucharest, 1991

Porumbăceanu Claudiu P., *La situation politique-administrative et la reinstauration de l'administration roumaine dans le departement de Satu-Mare*, in *Transylvanian Review*, no. 4, 1995

Pușcaș Vasile, *Al doilea Război Mondial. Transilvania și*

aranjamentele europene (1940 – 1944), Centrul de Studii Transilvane, Fundaţia Culturală Română, Cluj-Napoca, 1995

Puşcaş Vasile, *Speranţă şi disperare. Negocieri Româno-Aliate, 1943-1944*, Ed. Litera, Bucharest, 1995

Puşcaş Vasile, *National and territorial conflicts in Central and Eastern Europe and the Enforcement of Soviet Domination (1944-1947)*, in *Transylvanian Review*, 4, 1995

Quinlan D. Paul, *Ciocnire deasupra României. Politica Anglo-Americană faţă de România 1938-1947*, Centrul de Studii Româneşti, Fundaţia Culturală Română, Iaşi, 1995

Radosav Doru, *Donbas. O istorie deportată*, Ed. Ravensburg, 1994

Raimondo Craveri, *L'invasione sovietica dell'Europa e la Ressistenza*, Guida Editori, Napoli, 1986

Revisionism or Autonomy? Documents regarding the History of the Hungarian-Romanian Relations (1945-1947), Budapest, 1998

Romsics Ignac, *Wartime American Plans for a New Hungary and the Paris Peace Conference, 1941 – 1947* in *20th Century Hungary and the Great Powers*, Edited by Ignac Romsics, Central European University Press, New York, 1995

Romsics Ignac, Bela K. Kiraly, *Geopolitics in the Danube Region. Hungarian reconciliation efforts, 1848-1998*, Central European University Press, New York, 1999

Romsics Ignac, *Hungary in the Twentieth Century*, Budapest, 1999

Rupnik Jacques, *The other Europe*, Pantheon Books, New York, 1989

Sălăgean Marcela, *Northern Transylvania – October 1944 – March 1945. The Soviet Administration and its Problems*, in *Transylvanian Review*, no.1, 1995

Sălăgean Marcela, *Statutul juridic, administrativ şi politic al Transilvaniei de Nord, noiembrie 1944 – martie 1945*, in *Studii de istorie a Transilvaniei*, Cluj-Napoca, 1999

Sălăgean Marcela, *Considerations sur la presence des troupes sovietiques dans la Transylvanie du Nord*, in *Transylvanian Review*, no.4, 1996

Schpflin George, *Politics in Eastern Europe*, 1945 – 1992, Oxford, 1993

Scurtu Ion, Hlihor Constantin, *Complot împotriva României 1939 – 1947*, Bucharest, 1994

Sovietizarea Nord-Vestului României (1944-1950), Ed. Muzeului Sătmărean, Satu-Mare, 1996

Şandru Dumitru, *Ukrainean Nationalists, the Maramureş and Bukovina*, in *Transylvanian Review*, no.4, 1996

Şandru Dumitru, *Regimul cetăţeniei locuitorilor din Nordul Transilvaniei*, in *Sovietizarea Nord-Vestului României 1944-1950*, Ed. Muzeului Sătmărean, Satu-Mare, 1996

Şandru Dumitru, *Jandarmeria româna. 1944-1945*, in *Arhivele Totalitarismului*, no. 3, 1994

6 Martie 1945,începuturile comunizării României, Ed. Enciclopedică, Bucharest, 1995

Şef Rabin Dr. Moses Rosen, *Primejdii, incercări, miracole*, Ed. Hasefer, Bucharest, 1990

Şuţa Ion, *România la cumpăna istoriei*, August '44, Ed. Ştiinţifică, Bucharest, 1991

The lessons of Yalta, editor Pompiliu Teodor, Presa Universitară Clujeană, Cluj-Napoca, 1998

*Transilvania văzută în publicistica istorică maghiară. Momente din istoria Transilvaniei apărute în revista **Historia***, Ed. Pro-Print, Miercurea-Ciuc, 1999

Transylvania. The roots of Ethnic Conflict, Ed. John F. Cadzov, Louis J. Elteto, Kent State University Press, Kent, Ohio, 1983

Traşcă Ottmar, *15 octombrie 1944 – eşecul încercării Ungariei de a încheia armistiţiu*, in *Sovietizarea Nord-Vestului României (1944-1945)*, Satu-Mare, 1996

Ţârău Virgil, *Problema naţională în politica Partidului Comunist Român în anii 1944 – 1946. Consideraţii preliminare*, in *Anuarul Institutului de Istorie Cluj-Napoca*, 1997

Ţârău Virgil, *Le probleme nationale dans la politique du Parti Communiste Roumain entre 1944 – 1945*, in *Transylvanian Review*, no. 4, 1996

Ţârău Virgil, *Dezvoltarea structurilor de putere ale Partidului Comunist Român în judeţul Cluj: 1945-1946*, in *Anuarul Institutului de Istorie*, Cluj, XXX/1993

Vesa Vasile, *The Yalta Conference and the Institution of the Government Led by dr. Petru Groza*, in *Transylvanian Review*, no. 4, 1995

Vesa Vasile, *Conferinţa de la Yalta şi instaurarea guvernului condus de Petru Groza, in 6 Martie 1945. Începuturile comunizării României*, Ed. Enciclopedică, Bucharest, 1995

Vesa Vasile, *România şi Italia la conferinţa de pace din anii 1946-1947*, in *Studia Universitatis Babeş-Bolyai, Historia*, 1-2, year XXVI, 1991

Vesa Vasile, Marcela Sălăgean, *From Soviet Administration in Transylvania to Nationalist Frictions in the Relations between Romanian and Hungarian Communists*, in *Romanian and British historians on the contemporary history of Romania*, Edited by George Cipăianu and Virgiliu Ţârău, Cluj University Press, 2000

Vescan Teofil, *Situaţia din Nordul Ardealului*, in *Scânteia*, the 25th of January 1945

Verona Sergiu, *Military Occupation and Diplomacy. Soviet Troops in Romania 1944 – 1958*, Duke University Press, Durham, London, 1992

Volt egyszer egy Des. Bethlem, Magyarlapos, Retteg, Nagyilonda es Kornyeke, vol.II, Tel-Aviv, P.O.B., 1969

Wartime American Plans for a New Hungary. Documents from the U.S. Department of State, 1942-1944, Columbia University Press, New York, 1992

APPENDICES

1. Bucharest, October the 18th, 1944; Directions for the organization and the operation of the volunteers detachments «Iuliu Maniu»

THE NATIONAL COMMITTEE FOR THE ENLISTMENT
AND THE ORGANIZATION OF THE VOLUNTEERS
FOR TRANSYLVANIA,
AT THE NEWSPAPER *ARDEALUL*

The Legion of Volunteers for Transylvania Buc. 18 Oct. 1944
«Iuliu Maniu»
THE HIGH COMMAND

We have the honour to inform You that, conformably to the operation directions of the Volunteers Legion for Transylvania, the Commands of the operative detachments are organized and function as follows:

1) The commander of the operative detachments: Prof. Leon Bochiş

2) The battlefield military office:

office's chief: Colonel Eng. Cornel Boban as commander assistant

secretary: Major C. Dudescu

The battlefield military office represents the leadership of all the detachments now in training or in the battlefield of the Volunteers Legion, the training, the supervision, guidance and inspection of which being its competence in all respects from a military point of view.

Any other previous disposition is null and void.

Also, as for the military operations concerning the volunteers, the commander and the military office are to perform precisely and immediately the order no. 67610 of the General Head Quarters, section I/the 5th of October 1944.

The receiving and the fulfilling of the present order are to be reported.

At the same time, we warn you that you are to sanction any violation of the military laws and the cases that are under the sanctions of the penal code are to be investigated and, in addition to the hearing of the guilty person, the indited acts are to be forwarded to the respective

Court Martial, aware of the fact that both the commander and the battlefield military office alone bear the responsibility for the actions of the volunteers on the battlefield.

The commander and the military office have the duty to give us notice of every cases, in order to be known by the Central Command of the Volunteers Legion for Transylvania.

Herewith this order, we also send you an exemplary of the directions for the organization and the operation of the committee and the command for Transylvania.

We ask you that the stipulations of the present order and also the organization directions are to be immediately brought to the knowledge of every volunteers detachment, by order of the day.

The volunteer ladies are subjected to the same conditions with the volunteers, all of them being subjected to the same common conditions stipulated by the order of the General HeadQuarters no. 67610/1944

President and Commander
of the legions
of the Volunteers
for Transylvania «Iuliu Maniu»

s.s. Dr. Anton Ion Mureşanu

General Secretary
and Commander
of the Operations
of Enlistment and Organization

Ion Groşanu

The Central Historical National Archives
Fund «Ministerul Afacerilor Interne, Direcţia Administraţiei de Stat»
Dos. 19/1944

2. Bucharest, January 1945; Report concerning the activity of the volunteers detachments «Iuliu Maniu». Measures taken with the view of their dissolving.

The statement of Major Dudescu, from which the following are resulting:

The volunteers corps for Transylvania has been created by Mr. Leon Bochiş, Inspector I.N.C., Ioan Groşanu editor at the newspaper «Ardealul» and Professor Gabriel Ţepelea...

Finding on the spot extremely serious things, I have returned in Bucharest and I have reported to Colonel Zamfirescu, chief of the First Section of the General Head Quarters.

Of the declaration of the reserve Sub-lieutenant Gheorghe Togan, found in the file no. 4, it has been ascertained that the initiators of the Volunteers Corps are Ioan Groşanu, Leon Bochiş and Gabriel Ţepelea, the Commanders of the volunteers detachments have been appointed by Ioan Groşanu, while Dr. Anton Ionel Mureşanu and Ioan Groşanu have signed all the papers calling themselves «Commanders», the register with all the cashing has been kept by Ioan Groşanu.

From the report no. 119943 of the 28th of December 1944 of the General Head Quarters, Section I, Office 3, The mobilization of the Army, sent to the Office of the Ministry of War, it results that,

About the incidents produced by the units of Transylvanian volunteers in northern Transylvania, though the General Head Quarters has taken action in order to dissolve them, it is still informed by some Army's units that the newspaper «Ardealul» keeps on issuing various certificates for the volunteers that have already been disbanded and discharged.

It has been put up at the newspaper «Ardealul» and there have been taken all the stamps and the printed forms related to the enlistment of the Transylvanian volunteers, on the 3rd of January 1945 by Mr. Military Examining Att., Lt.-Magistrate Grigorescu Victor.

The Central Historical National Archives
Fund «Ministerul Afacerilor Interne, Direcţia Administraţiei de Stat»
Dossier 19/1944

3. Sibiu, December the 9th, 1944; The situation of the volunteers regiments

Report HUGHUES, MAGURA to the General Head Quarters General Mardari

There is no clear account of the volunteers detachments that operated in Transylvania, because there was not an one-man command, it is not known how many detachments there were, not all of them have operated with the Fourth Army's knowledge and even more yet, it seems that isolated elements under the form of bands still operate in northern Transylvania, that Lt. Colonel Bobancu, deceiving the good faith of the General Head Quarters, has set himself up for being, at the time, Commander of the Volunteers Detachment, then Commander of the Regiment «Iuliu Maniu» and, finnaly, liquidator of the Volunteers detachments and from the declaration of Lt. Colonel Bobancu, it results that he was attracted by the propaganda of the newspaper «Ardealul» for volunteer enlistment and admitted that, after he took the command of the Volunteers Detachment II, he has left to Sibiu and has also taken the command of the Volunteers Detachment III, afterwards taking the command of yet another Volunteers Detachment, he was guided by the Fourth Army to Alba Iulia. Lt. Colonel Bobancu also admits that most of the officers and corporals had false ranks and on the 6th of October 1944, he received the address no. 3200 of the newspaper «Ardealul», by means of which it is brought to his knowledge that he has been appointed Commander of the Regiment «Iuliu Maniu», that newspaper ensuring him that his appointment was established by the General Head Quarters and he was informed that he should take care of the Volunteers Detachment IV and V, too, both of them sent to the Fourth Army.

Also, from the report mentioned above, drawn up by MAGURA, it results that a disgracefully bad recruitment has been made, of all the detachments that have been organized with chiefs having a past of the worse and that it also results robberies and disorders committed by these detachments.

This report drawn up by MAGURA for the General Head Quarters has been given under the no. 108.180 of the 9th of December 1944 and it has been registered at the Prosecuting Magistracy of the Territorial Court Martial C.VI. Sibiu to the Territorial VI Corps.

The Central Historical National Archives
Fund «Ministerul Afacerilor Interne. Direcţia Administraţiei de Stat»
Dossier 19/1944

4. Bucharest, December the 12th, 1944; Investigation carried out in northern Transylvania – November 1944

12 DEC. 1944

GENERAL, SIR,

As a result of Mr. Chairman of the Council's letter, no. 1826 from the 19th of November 1944 and as an answer to Your address no. V-250 from the 28th of November 1944, I have the honour to give You the following information regarding the stage of the investigation carried out in northern Transylvania and the results obtained until now:

1) Prior to the 16th of November 1944, the Romanian civil authorities have been evacuated from the northern Transylvanian territory. There have left, at the request of the Soviet military authorities, a few teams of the Romanian Railways in order to rehabilitate the deteriorated railroads, also some postal services.

2) According to the order of the General Head Quarters no. 71202 from the 13th of November 1944, it has been ordered the immediate withdrawal of the military formation's troops from northern Transylvania (Territorial circles, Gendarmes Legions, firefighters, units).

3) According to the order no. 71215 from the 12th of November 1944, the General Head Quarters has taken action for the suppression of all the volunteers units that have operated in the framework of the large units on the battlefront. By the order no. 720622 from the 18th of November 1944, it has been decided the identification and the immediate dissolution on the spot of the paramilitary formations.

General St. Vinogradov, Esq.,
Vice-President
of the Control Commission

The Archive of the Ministry of Foreign Affairs
Dossier *Transilvania*/1944-1945
vol. 139 *Comisia Aliata de Control*

5. Bucharest, December the 24th, 1944; The surveillance of every publication that appear within the territory of the district of Mureş

Bucharest,
24 XI 1944

MINISTRY OF INTERNAL AFFAIRS
- THE PRESS DEPARTMENT-
NO. 13.444/25 XI, 1944

CIRCULAR ORDER
for
THE PREFECT'S OFFICE OF THE DISTRICT OF *MURES*

Conformably to the comunique sent to this Department by the Director for the Press and Information from the Ministry of Foreign Affairs, it is being brought to your knowledge for information and execution the following:

1) You are to comunicate immediately the Department for the Press and information from the Ministry of Foreign Affairs – Bucharest, st. N. Filipescu, no. 40, a list with the new daily or periodical publications that appear throughout your district, in which it should be specified the number and the date of the publication license and who has given the respective license.

2) Until the receiving of the licenses from the Political Department of the Allied Control Commission, the publications of the political parties and the independent newspapers, that offers certainty that they militate in the framework of the present political ideas, may appear in a provisional manner.

3) You are to warn all the publications within your district that they are to send, immediately and regularly, to the Department for the Press and Information from the Ministry of Foreign Affairs – Bucharest, st. N. Filipescu, no. 40 – 10 copies of every issue, copies required by the control exerted by the Allied Control Commission.

CABINET DIRECTOR
Petre Popovici

The Romanian National Archives – Tg-Mureş
Fund «Prefectura Judeţului Mureş»
Dossier 348/1944

6. Bucharest, November the 24th, 1944; Measures concerning the assistance and the repatriation of the Soviet citizens

MINISTRY OF FOREIGN AFFAIRS
The Administration General Secretary's office
no. 00321 – 24 Nov 1944

THE PREFECT'S OFFICE OF THE DISTRICT OF *MURES*

Finding that not all the district prefect's offices have complied exactly to the comunicated normative dispositions, with regard to the fulfiling of the art. 5 of the Convention of Armistice, concerning the assistance and the repatriation of the Soviet citizens, we ask you to be willing to inform your subordinate structures charged with the execution of the measures of assistance and repatriation of the Soviet citizens to comply strictly and completely with the given orders, comunicatted under the no. 3172 /the 7th of October, 3702/the 15th of November and 3865/the 17th of November crt.

Therefore, you are to supervise the registration of the Soviet citizens with the view of their repatriation, their accomodation in good conditions, the medical assistance they are entitled to, the payment of their food allowance and of the clothing indemnity, the measures of entraining and the organization of the transportation and the precise achievement of the requested workings.

The district prefect's office are to forward immediately nominal lists with all the Soviet citizens registered with the view of their repatriation, on the address of the Special Service for Redressation. Allies. from the Ministry of Internal Affairs, st. Theodor Aman, no. 12, Bucharest.

These lists will include all the data regarding the identity of the Soviet citizens and will make mention of the ammounts payed to them – in order to remove any possible wrongs in the payment of the pecuniary rights attributted to the Soviet citizens, by the eventual effectuation of the payment twice, in the countryside and in the Capital.

In this way, it is being drawn the attention of all Soviet citizens established in the countryside that, by mutual agreement with the Soviet Control Commission from Bucharest, it has been decided that all the Soviet citizens registered for repatriation are compelled to remain in the localities where they find at the moment, until the effectuation of the embarkation and their transportation...

GENERAL SECRETARY
MAGISTRATE COLONEL

The Romanian National Archives – Tg-Mureş
Fund «Prefectura Judeţului Mureş»
Dossier 5/1944

7. Cluj, December the 7th, 1944; Problems faced by the Romanian refugees at their return in the city

INFORMATIVE NOTE NO. 178
from 7. XII. 1944

We are informed that, as a result of the removal of the administrative authorities from northern Transylvania, a great concern is noticed among the refugees from that territory, it is being accused the Hungarian element that it tries, by cheating, to rule over that territory definitively, under the protection of the allied troops.

Some of the refugees, returning home to see theirs abandoned properties, have been chased away by force by the Hungarian guards that patrol armed the cities and the villages under the protection of the occupation troops, pretending that the ones coming from Romania are fascists and that they remain in those regions only for the purpose of spying.

The population of German origin has coalesced with the Hungarians, taking part at meeting and speeches in German language, disregarding the fact that a great number of their conationals are recruited in or fled with the German troops.

The fled Romanian inhabitants, seeing this state of affairs, express their desperation, as they are chased away once more from their abandoned homes.

Certain Information

The Commander
of the C.F.R. Gendarmes Legion
Lt. Colonel,
Gh. Stănescu

The Chief of the Police
and Security Office
Captain
M. Constantinescu

Comunique:
I.G.J. Dir. Sig. si O.P.

The Central Historical National Archives
Fund «Inspectoratul General al Jandarmeriei»
Dossier 35/1945

8. Bucharest, December the 22nd, 1944; Measures of calling in some publications

The General Inspectorate of the Gendarmerie
The Department of Security and Public Order

CIRCULAR ORDER No. 50.428
from the 22nd of December 1944

Respectfully it is transmitted below the copy of the order from the Ministry of Internal Affairs – Department for Documentation and Administrative Studies no. 111.259/944, concerning the application of the 16th article of the Armistice Convention, the matter of which we ask you to consider and command the accurate carrying out.

D.O.

The Director
of the Security
and Public Order
Lt. Colonel S. TEODORESCU

COPY: of the order M. of Internal Aff. No. 111.259/944

About the application of the 16th article of the Armistice Convention, you are to take the following measures:

The periodical or non-periodical publications, which are detrimental through their contents to our good relations with the Allies, are to be called in.

The medals and the metallic badges, carrying similar inscriptions or aspects, are to be collected and sent to the district's Prefect's Office, from where they will be sent to the National Mint for melting.

The list with the forbidden publications (publishing houses, printing houses, bookstores, authors with their own publishing house, public institutions and private enterprises) is to be handed to the Prefect's Offices...

In the public libraries with legal bailment and in the libraries of the superior education institutions, these publications are to be called in, inventoried and locked in boxes or in special rooms and kept under strict surveillance and on their own responsability and only inside the library's building.

For the exact fulfilment of the Armistice Convention's stipulations, you are to take steps so that the subordinated structures will check out if the public and private organizations mentioned in the order above still hold forbidden publications.

Certify this is a true copy
The Chief of the Security Office I
Captain, M. C. DUTA

The Romanian National Archives – Bistriţa
Fund «Legiunea de Jandarmi Năsăud»
Dossier 10/1944-1945

9. Oradea, February the 8th, 1945; Report concerning the Hungarian People's Union from Romania

No.378
1945, Month II, Day 8

THE GENERAL INSPECTORATE OF THE GENDARMERIE
«The Department for Security and Public Order»

As a result of the Informative Note No. 60/08.01.1945 given by this Inspectorate and the Informative Note No. 215/26.01.1945 with regard to the so called Hungarian organization «The Hungarian People's Union from Romania» that, from the investigation done, we found that it is nothing but the organization «Madosz».

I have the honour to report that on the 1st of February, the citizen Şipoş from the village Tinca, district of Bihor, has presented at the Gendarmes Legion Bihor, as being the representative of the above mentioned organization, pretending that it is a legally constituted organization and that it is part of the «Patriotic Defense».

At the Gendarmes Legion of Bihor has also showed up the president of the Patriotic Defense from Beiuş, a person called Ritz, that has pretended, too, that this organization is part of the Patriotic Defense, so that it has all the freedom of expression, the same with any other democratic party. As in this organization, the majority of the adherents are inhabitants of Hungarian ethnic origin and they are secretely carrying on an irredentist Hungarian activity, as it has been reported with the above informative notes, we ask you to be willing to inform us whether this organization may or may not function.

GENDARMES INSPECTORS ORADEA
COLONEL,
Alex. V. Ionescu

The Chief of the Political Service
Captain

The Central Historical National Archives
Fund «Inspectoratul General al Jandarmeriei»
Dossier 35/1945

10. Oradea, February the18th, 1945; The position of the Hungarians towards the removal of the Romanian administration from northern Transylvania

The problem: The Hungarian Irredenta

INFORMATIVE NOTE No. 381
from the 18th of February 1945

For some time now, among the inhabitants of Hungarian ethnic origin in this legion's territory it has been noticed a vivid satisfaction and that is because of the fact that northern Transylvania has not been rendered to Romania even until now, the administration of the territory is Hungarian, too, while in various regions there are arriving soldiers in Hungarian military uniforms and armed.

Besides all these, it adds further on and contributes the fact that the Soviet soldiers are more time in the entourage of the Hungarian inhabitants while towards the Romanians they have a hostile attitude and cavil at them.

- Certain Information –

Reported:
Bihor I.G.J. THE GENDARMES LEGION'S COMMANDER

Inspect. Jd. Oradea
Comand. G-l al Etapelor Nr. 2
Prefectura Jud. Bihor

The Central Historical National Archives
Fund «InspectoratulGeneral al Jandarmeriei»
Dossier 35/1945

11.Oradea, February 1945; The establishment of the Hungarian People's Union in the village of Arpăşel, district of Bihor.

The Activity of the Hungarian Irredenta

In the village of Arpăşel, district of Bihor, it has been constituted the Hungarian organization called «The Hungarian People's Union from Romania» (Romaniai magyar nepszoveseg).

To this organization have adhered, until now, approximately 240 Hungarian inhabitants, 40 women among them.

Each member is paying a monthly subscription of 60 lei and it is being issued for him a member card.

Among the Hungarian inhabitants from the district of Bihor there is some talk of the manner to get an approval so that the administrative authorities from the Hungarian villages would use only the Hungarian language.

Certain Information

The Central Historical National Archives
Fund «Inspectoratul General al Jandarmeriei»
Dossier 35/1945

12. Bucharest, December the 13th, 1944; The addresses exchanged between General Rădescu and Marshal Malinovsky with regard to the setting up of the Romanian administration in Transylvania.

The Political Dep. Bucharest, the 13th of December 1944
116.074

General, Sir,

On referring to Your address No. 683169/02.12, I have the honour to inform you that simultaneously with the address exchange between Adjutant-General Rădescu and Marshal Malinovsky that you were willing to give me in copy, an exchange of notes has taken place between Adjutant-General Sănătescu, at the time Chairman of the Council of Ministers, and Marshal Vinogradov, Vice-President of the Allied Control Commission, concerning the question of the introduction of the Romanian administration in Transylvania.

Herewith I have the honour of giving you in copy the address from the 28th of November 1944, No. V. 250 of General Vinogradov to General Sănătescu. In this address, the Control Commission is adopting a point of view less rigid in this problem. It shows, as a conclusion, that the question of the Romanian administration's installation in the northern Transylvanian territory is to be settled by the negotiations with the U.S.S.R.'s government. Mr. C. Vişoianu, Minister of Foreign Affairs, has pointed out the distinction between the points of view comprised in the note of General Vinogradov.

TO THE GENERAL SECRETARY
CHIEF OF THE GENERAL HEADQUARTERS

The archive of the Ministry of Foreign Affairs
Dossier «Transilvania»/1944-1945, vol.139. C.A.C.

13. Cluj, December the 1st, 1944; Rumours about the Soviet Union's intentions towards the Romanian frontiers

the 1st of December 1944
No. 482

In Cluj there are some rumours going about the new politics of the U.S.S.R. These rumours have passed the border of the Feleac and are being discussed very vehemently in the Romanian circles of Turda. It is being said that they are even the matter for discussions within the party clubs. These rumours are said to have a real cause and they would come from Soviet sources.

The Soviet Union would intend to create the Republic of Dobrudja, together with the Danube's mouths, with the capital at Constanţa. The small republic thus created, unable to exist by its own democratic government, would ask the joining, that is the annexation, to U.S.S.R.

It is being reported that the U.S.S.R. would have asked Romania to cede of its own accord the Danube's mouths and the coastline, that is Dobrudja, in return for northern Transylvania, that the Romanian government would have refused that thing, so that they try now the diversion with the Dobrudjan Republic.

The U.S.S.R., it is being said, would want that at the Peace Conference, they would find certain achievements «by mutual agreement», that is, with the things accomplished.

The Romanian National Archives Cluj-Napoca
Fund «Biroul de Cenzură Cluj – Turda»
Dossier 9/1944-1945

14. Cluj, December the 2nd, 1944; Actions of compromising the Bucharest governments, committed within the Romanian territory

the 2nd of December 1944
No. 484

The robberies, the misdeeds, the maltreating and the cruelties that are committed throughout the country aim one purpose: the compromising of the governments that succeed each other and which, are not, any of them, to the liking of the dominators, creating dissatisfactions and riots, if possible, in order to show that the Romanian governments are not able neither to maintain the order inside the country, nor to satisfy the conditions imposed by the armistice treaty.

In this manner, it gives the chance to a double intervention: respecting the armistice's conditions and ensuring the order within the country, as a consequence, thus, the military occupation of Romania by the Soviets, creating a pro-Soviet government and declaring Romania as integral part of the U.S.S.R.

To all these obvious intentions of the Soviets, the British and the Americans would say, anyway, that it has not come the time yet and that we must wait and suffer, just like Czechoslovakia, Poland and Yugoslavia. The right time has not come yet.

The painful thing is that the Communist Party and its annexes are playing in an evil and treacherous manner so that a foreign power would do everything to accomplish its plans of destroying the small nations.

In these circumstances and in this tragically overwhelming atmosphere the Romanian public and the Romanian conscience are expressing their helplessness to take action. This will is asking for no more than one call and every one, absolutely every single one, intellectuals and workers, would stand for our motherland's defence.

This is the way we have seen the Romanian public opinion and this is the way we convey it.

The Romanian National Archives Cluj-Napoca
Fund «Biroul de Cenzură Cluj-Turda»
Dossier 9/1944-1945

15. Cluj, December the 2nd, 1944; The Romanian reactions to the military developments in the Hungarian territory. Possible frontier modifications.

The 2nd of December 1944
No. 485

alarming news are announcing us:

- The Soviet Army has been repulsed on the middle battlefront up to Cernăuţi, on the southern battlefront up to Solnoc, where, between Sojol and Debrecen, it has formed a bridge head over Tisa. (It is thus obvious why the maps under discussion are giving to the Romanians this part of territory in return for the Danube's mouths, Dobrudja, Maramureş and Banat.)

The Romanian public of that region is commenting with anxiety upon these events. Some are saying that the Soviets are deliberately ceding territory in the north and in the south so that the Romanian divisions from Tokai-Csap and the surroundings would be captured, in order to force Romania to adopt the baneful politics of the destructive communism.

It is being commented a lot also upon the rumour that, given that situation, the Soviets would have asked for help to the British and the Americans, who are ready to give their assistance in return for the declaration that the British – American's influence extends upon all the European countries, including the Balkans and the Romanians. In return for this declaration, the British and the Americans would help out with the Balkans Army, but not with armament.

The Romanian public opinion is very concerned. Even the peasants that come from the countryside are making all kinds of disconcerting prophecies.

The Romanian National Archives Cluj-Napoca
Fund «Biroul de Cenzură Cluj-Turda»
Dossier 9/1944-1945

16. Cluj, January the 3rd, 1945; Rumours that went around the inhabitants of northern Transylvania, on the eve of the signing of the armistice between Hungary and the Soviet Union. Frontier changes in Central Europe.

The 3rd of January 1945
No. 503

About the recent developments from Hungary and the leaving to Moscow of a Hungarian government's delegation from Debrecen for the conclusion of a treaty between the Hungarians and the Russians, the rumours that come to us from beyond the Feleac are as alarming as can be. They produce among the Romanian population on the both sides of the Feleac a real shock. More and more often are heard exclamations of the type: «The Romanian troops are fighting with all possible strength, are unselfishly sacrificing themselves and have remarkable real successes – fact non-recognized by the allies – while the Romanians are more and more oppressed, there are required to them sacrifices impossible to achieve, the Romanian economy is destroyed, the order is threatened, the country's independence is a fiction, the Hungarians are protected by our allies, in spite of the fact that they are fighting in the enemy's line.

One of our informers, recently arrived from Oradea Mare, is informing us that the Hungarian leading circles from that region are very optimist with regard to the future of Hungary and the Hungarians. He has declared approximately the following:

The delegation that went to Moscow for the armistice treaty will achieve the maximum of the secret Hungarian – Russian treaty's conditions of the autumn of 1942. These are the following main points, says the Hungarian collocutor:

In return for the help Hungary would give to the Soviets by the joining of the Hungarian troops to the allies the moment the Soviet troops would have reached the Carpathians and by forming a front in the rear of the Romanian – German front, Hungary should have obtained:

- Southern Transylvania up to the border of the Bucharest treaty, Oltenia up to west of Craiova;
- Croatia, part of Slovenia with Fiume;
- Part of Carinthia and Austria;

- Territorial rectifications in Slovakia and Ruscinsco;
- Free zone at the Black Sea.

The events of August 1944 and Sallasi's coup d'etat have overthrown the plans of the Hungarian democrats.

Now, the Moscow's delegation would have to get the best of that moment's conditions.

- We know, says the Hungarian collocutor, that the way the events are already taking place in the field, Moscow would not admit Romania's sovereignty over the territories from beyond the Carpathians, not even if Romania would become a Soviet republic. Romania is not able to fulfil the conditions of the armistice treaty. The extension of the Debrecen government's sovereignty over northern Transylvania will take place before the conclusion of the agreement between the Hungarians and the Russians, while the military occupation of southern Transylvania is just a matter of time.

*

On the other hand, there are some rumours, also on the Hungarian part, that the Debrecen government is the emanation of the London Hungarian one and that, with the approval of Sallasi and the Germans, it is supposed to obtain from the Russians the arming of some discharged contingents. This army would play a major part the moment Russia will be attacked from East and South.

*

We have conveyed the rumours as we have received them. There is one thing that we could notice, anyway, within the public opinion: a depressing pessimism, close to despair.

The Romanian National Archives Cluj-Napoca
Fund «Biroul de Cenzură Cluj – Turda»
Dossier 9/1944-1945

17. Sighet, March the 12th, 1945; Secessionist actions of the Ruthenians and Ukraineans from Maramureş.

The 12th of March 1945
No. 569

The mountains of Maramureş are in rebellion. The news that a bunch of people alien to the Romanian nation have desecrated this part of the country has quickly spread and the news about the arresting of the Maramureş's National Council's leaders has filled the souls of Romanians with grief and anger.

The Ruthenians, in order to revenge on the Romanians for collecting over 70.000 signatures for the remaining of Maramureş to the Motherland, as they are extremely few, have left the authorities leadership to the hands of the Hungarians. Those Hungarians that a few weeks ago were arrested as partisans are now actually leading the district. The prefect is the Ruthenian Odolentchuk.

The Maramureş's Romanians, aware of the fact that there is freedom and that, on the basis of the convention of armistice, they have the right to decide their fates, have planned a rebellion, with the purpose of installing again Romanian leadership in their capital, Sighet, as it was in the beginning, that of the Romanian National Council, instead of the Ruthenian – Hungarian one, that installed itself by force.

Monday, the 5th of March 1945, from every corner of Maramureş, the Romanians have set out to Sighet in floods. For all contingencies, they have taken with them guns, too. The people from the Iza's Valley have had pistols, Bren guns and two machine guns, about ten thousands of them. The ones from the Vişeu's valley have come up armed with two cannons, two bomb-dropping guns, mines, grenades and 7 carts with ammunition and left word back home that, in case they are not returning within three days, they should send ten more carts with ammunition.

The twenty thousands people storm is getting close to Sighet. They halt near Petrova and Bârsana. They are waiting for news from the ones left from Mara and Tisa, that are late. Here they are doing firing tests, everything is working fine. They are heading for Sighet, slowly, in battle line.

Serious agitation in Sighet. The Romanian intellectuals are summoned and it is being said to them that they must stop the march, to guide the peasants to their homes, otherwise the Military Command would «consider» this march as being directed against the Army so that the army will fire and exterminate all Romanians as enemies.

A delegation of Romanians is coming on their way and, after long discussions, convince them and they return home.

The people from the Valleys of Mara and Tisa are arriving, meanwhile, with delay. They do not know what is going on on the other side, they reach Sighet. The road is blocked by the Army and the Ukrainean police, arrived at that moment.

Discussions began. The Army, in order to intimidate, is firing into the air, at the very moment the agreement is settled. The Ukrainean police (formed of civil guards) shoots to kill. A Jew from Sighet fires, too. There are two dead people and several wounded on the part of the Maramureş Romanians. The incident is closed due to the Romanian's reasonableness.

Afterwards, the arrestings have begun. Several dozens of intellectuals from Sighet and the district are arrested. They are imprisoned in the Sighet Prosecuting Office's jail.

The Romanian National Archives Cluj-Napoca
Fund «Biroul de Cenzură Cluj – Turda»
Dossier 9/1944-1945

18. Timişoara, February the 22nd, 1945; The statement of a student, native from Sighet, referring to the events that took place in Maramureş.

22.II.1945

Informative Note

On the 17. II. 1945 the student Kokesdy Ladislau from Sighet has come to the Security Office of the Police Station of Timişoara, willing to appear before the Population Office, showing a certificate issued by the National Council of Sighet. The above mentioned has come to Timişoara with the intention to enrol to the Polytechnic School of the city. He has declared, among other things, that while the mayor and the prefect of the district of Maramureş were gone to Bucharest with an official mission, a group of local inhabitants and N.K.V.D. members have entered in every house, forcing the population to subscribe to an act, telling that they want to join Ukraine. After the conclusion of the registration, by a majority vote, Maramureş has been proclaimed province attached to Ukraine, installing authorities to their own liking.

The Police Station . M of I. A.
To the Police Commissariate of Aiud

The Romanian National Archives Cluj-Napoca
Fund «Inspectoratul de Politie Cluj»
Dossier 397/1944-1945

19. Bistriţa, November the 24th, 1944; The situation of the district's elementary education.

Messrs Praetors to the *Residence*

As I have personally convinced myself, the elementary education has not started yet everywhere. Under the pretext that the school building could not be rehabilitated or that there are no teachers etc., nothing is being done, while with goodwill and a bit of energy a building could have been arranged in each village and, if not a schoolman, at least the village's priest could have taken care of the village's children two or three hours a day. Everybody is waiting for everything to be given to them in readiness, few people understand the exceedingly hard times and give their needed support.

I ask you to command that within 8 days, the elementary education to be resumed in every village, otherwise the mayors, the secretaries, the teachers and even the priests will be held responsible.

Bistriţa, on the 24th of Nov. 1944

Prefect

The Romanian National Archives Bistrita
Fund «Prefectura Judeţului Năsăud»
Dossier 263/1944

20. Oradea, March the 8th, 1945; Abuses committed on the occasion of the allotment of some inhabitants from the district of Bihor.

Problem: Information from Hungary

INFORMATIVE NOTE No. 529
from the 8th of March 1945

- In northern Transylvania, the Hungarian authorities have began the expropriation of the boyar's wealths to the peasants.

The estates larger than 15 hectares of tillable soil enter the expropriation plan.

The inhabitants that are not enroled in the «Ploughmen's Front» are not put in possession of land.

- The Schools Inspectorate of Oradea has appointed a volunteer from the division «Tudor Vladimirescu» as Romanian teacher in the village of Leş-Bihor.

At his arrival in the village, he has gathered all the inhabitants, forming two committees, one formed of men and the other formed of women, and they have discussed the question of the expropriation of the boyar's properties to the peasants.

The same teacher has forced the inhabitants to sign in a list, by telling them that through this they request the Romanian authorities to enter in northern Transylvania, while in fact, the list stipulated that the peasants are enroling of their own will in the «Ploughmen's Front».

- In some villages from northern Transylvania, the so-called «District Police» has assembled and it replaces the gendarmes. The people that form this police are dressed, part of them as civilians, part of them as soldiers and they are trying to persecute the Romanian element in every way.

Certain Information

The Commander
of the Bihor Gendarmes Legion
Major Marinaş Vasile

REPORTED
The General Inspectorate of the Gendarmerie
The Gendarmes Inspectorate Oradea
The General Command of the Stages
The Command of the Stages No. 2
The Prefect's Office of the District of Bihor

The Central Historical National Archives
Fund «Inspectoratul General al Jandarmeriei»
Dossier 35/1945